THE ART AND SCIENCE OF RACQUETBALL

Revised Second Edition

By
D. RAY COLLINS, Ed.D.
Professor of Physical Education
Department of Physical Education and Recreation
St. Cloud State University
St. Cloud, Minnesota

PATRICK B. HODGES, Ph.D.
Professor and Chairperson
Department of Physical Education and Athletics
Sinclair Community College
Dayton, Ohio

and

Michael G. Marshall, Ph.D.
Professional Kinesiologist

To our sons and daughters,

Jason Collins
Cathy Collins
Shaun Hodges
Shannon Hodges
Deborah Marshall
Rebekah Marshall
Kerry Marshall

Contents

Preface

People play racquetball for a number of reasons. Many participate in the sport primarily for health benefits, such as cardiovascular fitness and weight control. Some individuals thrive on the game as their way to satisfy a strong urge to compete against others. Still others view racquetball strictly in terms of its value as a meaningful recreational outlet, while countless numbers involve themselves in the sport for the purpose of receiving college credits. A few play the game well enough to make it their livelihood.

Whatever their motivation for playing racquetball, players inevitably share one common goal. They place a high priority on reaching full potential in this most enjoyable and exciting game. This is the mountaintop experience in racquetball. We hope that the contents of this book will be helpful to you in learning to play racquetball at your optimum proficiency. The book is designed for beginning and intermediate level players in educational institutions and racquetball clubs, but the more advanced performer in these settings could benefit from the book's contents, particularly the chapters dealing with stroke mechanics, racquetball injuries and strategy.

The book contains some features not commonly found in other instructional texts on racquetball. In our opinion, the text includes the most complete analysis of stroke mechanics presented in racquetball literature. Performance in the common racquetball strokes was filmed at 14 frames per second, with the key frames of each stroke sequence selected for presentation. We are confident that your study and application of this information will enable you to play closer to your potential.

The chapter on racquetball injuries provides information that will help you become less susceptible to certain injuries caused by poor stroke mechanics. Staying healthy is essential for you to play at peak performance.

The skills test items herein have several valuable applications. Instructors will find them useful for classifying students by ability level and as valuable teaching aids for checking student progress in skills development. Students can use them to monitor individual progress through self-testing. The test items can also be effectively used as practice drills. Achievement goals for each skill may be utilized by the instructor as a means for motivating the student. These goals would correspond with the instructor's course objectives.

Several people contributed to the development of this book. Our sincere thanks is extended to Dan Ferris for allowing us to capture his fluid stroke mechanics on film. The St. Cloud, Minnesota, native is currently recognized as the premier male amateur racquetball player in the United States.

We commend Mike Nelson of St. Cloud State University's instructional development unit for his excellent work in filming Dan Ferris' strokes. Also, we are indebted to the employees of the university's auxiliary services unit who transported equipment, provided special electrical services, and painted a racquetball court to prepare a proper setting for high-speed photography. Also, a special thank you to Canon U.S.A., Inc., Photographic Products Division, Elmhurst, Illinois, for the loan of the Canon High Speed F-1 Camera.

Pat Krueger deserves recognition for developing the many fine illustrations in the text. Gratitude is expressed to Ray's wife, Phyllis, for typing the manuscript in her usual competent fashion. A special thanks goes to the management of Front Wall Racquetball Club of St. Cloud, Minnesota, for providing the racquetball equipment pictorially displayed in the book.

D. Ray Collins
Patrick B. Hodges
Michael G. Marshall

1

Getting to Know Racquetball

Racquetball is one of the most popular recreational sports played today. A participant does not have to be a "super-athlete" or "pillar of strength" to actively engage in and enjoy racquetball competition. The fast-paced, strenuous game promotes positive physical and mental health for both men and women of all ages. Few sports can make that claim.

A phenomenal growth has occurred in the number of racquetball participants and facilities over the past several years in the United States. As early as 1970 there were 50,000 racquetball players in this country, and a professional tour had been established. Yet within a decade, more than eight million Americans were playing racquetball on the approximately 17,000 courts at the more than 800 clubs and numerous colleges and community service agencies available at that time. The demand for college racquetball classes is at an all-time high. The number taking up the game continues to grow each year as organizations such as the YMCA, YWCA, colleges and universities, secondary schools, health clubs and spas have found that racquetball courts are an absolute necessity to any financially successful operation.

Since racquetball is a fast-paced activity requiring only a short amount of time to obtain a vigorous workout, the game is a natural for today's physical fitness conscious generation. A measure of physical endurance, skill and total body control is required to play the game, and it is an excellent physical conditioning activity because of the demands placed on the player's cardio-respiratory system.

HISTORY

Tracing the game of racquetball from one particular origin is virtually impossible. It could be a descendant of a thirteenth century French game that resembled court tennis or maybe the seventh century Spanish game of jai alai. The eighteenth century British game of racquets is another possible forerunner, as well as the popular Irish game of handball. Most authorities seem to agree that racquetball, as it is played today, is a truly American game that evolved from the game of paddleball.

Earl Riskey is given credit for developing the original concept of paddleball and fostering the sport's growth while at the University of Michigan in the 1920s and 1930s. Apparently, he got the idea from watching tennis players practice various shots in a handball court. From his initial idea came the standardization

1

of the ball, wooden paddle and a set of rules. Paddleball was selected as one of the unofficial physical conditioners for the armed forces during World War II and continued to grow in popularity primarily at the YMCA organizations across the country. The increasing popularity of the sport led to the first national paddleball tournament, which was held in Madison, Wisconsin, in 1961.

Joe Sobeck is considered to be the "Father of Racquetball." While observing a group of paddleball players at the Greenwich, Connecticut, YMCA in 1949, he figured that the game could be improved by replacing the wooden racquets with a stringed racquet similar to a tennis racquet. He felt the stringed racquet, called a "paddle-racket," would enable the players to hit the ball with greater control and velocity, thus speeding up the pace of the game. The popularity of paddle-rackets spread quickly, and by 1965, Sobeck's new game was more popular than paddleball. The first national paddle-rackets tournament was held in Milwaukee, Wisconsin, in 1968.

The first international tournament for the new sport occurred one year later in St. Louis, Missouri. Two very important developments came from a meeting held at the tournament site. The official name of the game was changed from "paddle-rackets" to "racquetball." The second important development was the creation of the International Racquetball Association, with Robert Kendler assuming the role of president.

Kendler resigned as president of the International Racquetball Association in 1973 and was instrumental in forming the National Racquetball Club that same year. The National Racquetball Club sponsored a professional tour and conducted national tournaments for several years. The United States Racquetball Association was established a short time later and acted as the amateur arm of the National Racquetball Club. All three organizations are now defunct.

The national governing body for racquetball is the American Amateur Racquetball Association, a self-governing body administered by and for amateur racquetball players. This organization's monthly publication is entitled *Racquetball in Review*. The American Amateur Racquetball Association has been recognized by the United States Olympic Committee as the official ruling body of the sport.

EQUIPMENT AND SUPPLIES

Racquet

Racquetball racquets come in various sizes, shapes and colors. The basic design of a racquetball racquet is similar to that of a tennis racquet, but the racquetball racquet is much shorter and lighter. Your choice of racquet grip, weight and shape is extremely important and will directly affect your progress in skill development. Your selection of a racquet is a matter of personal preference, depending on such factors as strength, style of play and level of skill, as well as the seriousness with which you play the game.

Racquets are constructed from either metal, fiberglass or graphite, with each type of material having its unique strengths. These types of racquets vary greatly in flexibility or amount of resilience during the contact phase of the swing.

2

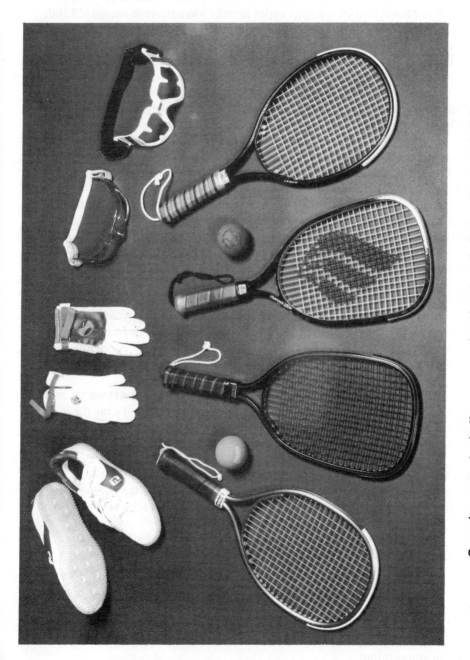

Sample racquets, balls, eye guards, gloves and shoes. Racquet head shapes, left to right: (1) oval (2) quadriform (3) rectangular (4) teardrop

3

The lighter graphite racquets display a high degree of flexibility for better touch and control. The metal and fiberglass racquets are less resilient. Racquet head shapes include the oval, quadriform, rectangular and teardrop designs.

The current cost of a racquet varies from $15 to a figure in excess of $200. Which racquet should you purchase? Unfortunately, no standard answer exists, since racquet selection is an individual matter. An expensive racquet that is ideally suited for one player may adversely affect the game of another player. The following may be helpful to you in selecting a racquet.

1. *Length* — The standard length of a racquet is 18 inches. Generally speaking, a longer racquet gives a player a little more control in performing a stroke and to a degree extends court coverage.

2. *Weight* — An important variable to consider. Most players are turning to the lighter weight racquets because they promote better control and quicker acceleration during the swing. The newer, more expensive racquets are as light as 235 grams, with the average weight around 250 grams.

3. *Grip* — Normally the grip is constructed of either rubber, leather or synthetics. The rubber grip is more durable and lasts longer, while the leather grip provides a more secure handhold.

The grip circumference is probably the most important variable you will need to consider when purchasing a new racquet. A grip that is too large or small for your hand size can negatively affect both your hitting power and control, thus significantly hindering your success in hitting the ball. Grip sizes range from 3 5/8 inches to 4 1/8 inches. If you have selected the proper grip, your two middle fingers should barely touch the palm when you wrap your fingers around the racquet grip. A common mistake is to get the grip size too large. A general rule is for men to use a small or medium grip with women using an extra small or small grip.

All racquets, regardless of grip size, should have a thong (loop of cord) attached to the base of the grip. As a safety measure, you should wrap the thong around your wrist during competition to prevent the racquet from slipping out of your hand.

4. *String* — Varies from the standard nylon to either gut, monofilament or graphite. String tension varies, depending on the type and quality of the racquet, but a racquet is normally strung between 24 and 32 pounds. Many of the higher-quality racquets are now strung a little tighter (33-35 lb.) to achieve greater shot velocity.

Most racquets are factory strung with nylon. The nylon string is durable, relatively inexpensive, and provides good ball control.

Ball

Racquetballs are manufactured by several companies and vary in price. Blue is the standard ball color, and the type used is determined by such factors as level of skill, style of game, sanctioning organization or individual preference. The American Amateur Racquetball Association has a recognized ball that is used in competition.

The rules specify that the ball should be 2.25 inches in diameter and should weigh approximately 1.4 ounces. Also, the height of its bounce should be

4

between 68 and 72 inches when dropped from a height of 100 inches at a temperature of 70 to 74 degrees Fahrenheit. Currently, about a half dozen brands meet the AARA specifications.

Accessories

1. *Eye guards* — This type of safety eyewear or other protective glasses, such as prescription athletic glasses, is definitely recommended, and is actually required for most tournaments. A racquetball can reach speeds in excess of 140 miles per hour, which makes the ball a dangerous flying object when a player is hit in the face, especially in an area as sensitive as the eye. It is not an uncommon occurrence for a ball to hit the edge of a racquet or for a player to simply lose control of a shot. Eye guards should be required equipment for all racquetball players from the beginner to the professional level. This inexpensive investment will certainly enable you to play with greater confidence and safety.

2. *Racquet guard* — This accessory, in the form of a strip of plastic, prolongs the life of your racquet and the walls of the racquetball court. Most racquetball organizations or clubs require racquet guards, and fortunately, most racquets come with a guard on the end of the racquet. If your racquet does not have one, a guard can be purchased inexpensively at most sporting goods stores. Some racquet guards are built into the frame and are replaced when racquets are restrung.

3. *Gloves* — An optional accessory. The glove assists in maintaining a dry, firm grip, which helps to promote proper shot control. The glove should be lightweight and thin so you can maintain the "feel" of the racquet. Most gloves are leather and can be cleaned through a normal washing procedure. Individuals who play on a regular basis normally own two or three pairs of gloves and change them after each game or match to insure dryness.

4. *Wearing apparel* — No definite rules apply as to what you should wear in competition other than that the clothes should be safe and comfortable. Racquetball shirts are normally lightweight T-shirts or the V-neck type. Shorts commonly worn in physical education classes are appropriate to wear, as well as the normal summer shorts. Most racquetball establishments and sporting goods stores sell racquetball outfits that are attractive, safe and comfortable.

Your choice of socks should be the regular white athletic type, and the tennis or racquetball shoe designed specifically for hard surfaces and quick foot movements is the proper shoe selection. Shoe design is an important variable in racquetball, as a good quality, snugly fit shoe can help prevent sore feet, blisters and sprained ankles.

Other optional accessories include a cloth wristband or headband that helps combat the problem resulting from perspiration of the hands and forehead area. Having a towel or other similar piece of cloth handy to wipe the perspiration from your face and arms during time-outs or between games is a good idea.

COURT DESIGN

Racquetball can be played on one-, three-, or four-wall courts. One- and three-wall courts are primarily located in the Sun Belt section of the country. Four-wall courts are by far the most prevalent and popular type of court. Our discussion in this book focuses on the four-wall court, an enclosed court with a ceiling. However, keep in mind that the principles of four-wall racquetball generally apply to the one- and three-wall games.

The walls and ceilings of racquetball courts are constructed from various materials, the most popular being either cement or prefabricated panels. Most floors are made of wood and are covered by a sealant, which gives a glossy appearance. Many of the newer courts have a special plexiglass back wall for instructional or observational purposes. Virtually all courts have some type of viewing area, which is normally located at the upper level of the back court. In large metropolitan areas or racquetball "hotbeds," racquetball facilities commonly contain one or more courts that are constructed with glass walls. These courts are surrounded by bleachers that can seat as many as 300 to 500 spectators and are specially designed for tournament play at both the amateur and professional levels.

The following diagram shows a regulation four-wall racquetball court with official measurements and court markings.

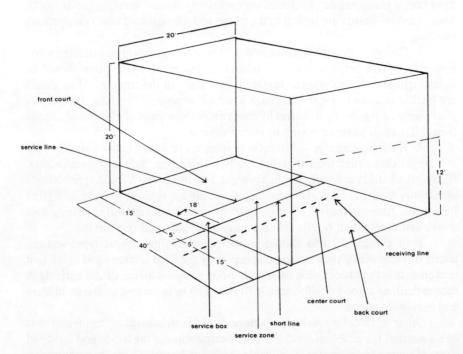

Four-wall racquetball court dimensions and markings (note optional observation area in back wall design).

OVERVIEW OF RACQUETBALL

Basic Rules

Racquetball can be played by two, three or four players. The game of singles is a fast-paced game that requires two opposing players to hit the ball on an alternating basis. Cutthroat involves three players, with the server playing against the other two competitors. In cutthroat, the server must hit the ball every other time, but either of the other two players may hit the alternate ball. Since cutthroat involves two players against one, it requires a little more strategy than singles and a greater emphasis on shot selection. However, it too is a fast-paced, exciting game. Doubles competition involves four players (two versus two). Careful shot selection is required, along with a great deal of strategy and teamwork.

In singles play, the game begins with the server standing in the service zone, usually near the middle of that court area. The server drops (bounces) and hits the ball in a manner so that it strikes the front wall first. To be considered a legal serve, the ball must touch the floor in the back court (behind the short line) before striking the back wall. A serve may hit one side wall after hitting the front wall as long as the ball lands in the back court before hitting a second side wall, the ceiling or the back wall. When the first serve's front wall rebound hits one of these surfaces, it is then a service fault and the server is allowed one more service attempt. Two successive faults result in a side-out, and the server then becomes the receiver.

The receiver should be positioned in the middle of the back court, approximately five feet away from the back wall. He/she may hit the ball after it crosses the five-foot line (receiving line) either in the air (volley) or after it hits the floor in the back court. The ball may bounce on the floor only one time, since a second bounce results in a dead ball and a point for the server. The receiver's primary objective is to return the ball to the front wall, but unlike the serve, the ball may strike any other wall (including the ceiling) before it hits the front wall. After the serve, the ball is alternately hit by each player (rally) until a dead ball results. (For a complete set of racquetball rules, refer to the Appendix.)

Scoring

Unlike games with related scoring systems, a racquetball game played under official rules ends when one player or team scores 15 points, which means there are no overtimes or two-point win rules. A final score can be 15-14. A match is considered to be the best two out of three games, with the last or third game, if necessary, limited to 11 points. Only the server can score points, and it is possible for a server to score 15 consecutive points without the receiver ever getting a chance to serve.

Modified scoring systems include the best three out of five 11-point games, three out of five 21-point games, scoring on every point exchange and a two-point win rule.

Safety and Etiquette

Racquetball is an enjoyable game in which you and your opponents can obtain a strenuous workout in a recreational setting. The word "opponent" should not imply the enemy but should instead mean a player with a common competitive interest. The words "competition" and "opponent" should be viewed in a positive sense, and a mutual feeling of trust and respect should be an integral part of every game.

Observing a few simple rules related to racquetball safety and etiquette will make the game more enjoyable for you and certainly a great deal safer.

Safety

1. Always allow your opponent plenty of room to complete a full swing, including his/her follow-through. Even though your maneuverability is somewhat restricted due to the court size, you still are responsible for getting out of the way of your opponent's racquet. If for some reason you feel your opponent is "too close for comfort" when you are preparing to hit the ball, do not swing. Simply call a hinder, and the ball will be put into play again with a serve. (Additional hinder rules are presented in the Appendix.)

2. Always allow your opponent a clear shot to the front wall. Remember to position yourself to the side or behind your opponent without removing yourself completely from the critical playing area. Give him/her a reasonable space or a "hitting alley." If your opponent is directly in front of your hitting area, do not swing at the ball. Each of you must make a reasonable attempt to get out of the other's way. Otherwise, an avoidable hinder may be called, and the point is automatically awarded to the server or a side-out occurs, depending on the situation and who committed the hinder.

3. Concentration is the key word to describe the basic requirement in any fast-paced, competitve game, especially racquetball. Always be aware of your position as well as the position of your opponent. In every game situation, learn to anticipate your opponent's next movement. Collisions and body contact will never be totally eliminated, but the problem can be greatly reduced simply by improving your power of concentration during play.

4. Eye injuries commonly occur in racquetball. The majority of these injuries are caused by the ball striking the eye. Proper court positioning will greatly reduce your chances of sustaining an eye injury. Another safety precaution, in addition to wearing the previously discussed eye guards, is to avoid watching your opponent hit the ball during the moment of actual contact. You should develop the habit of watching your opponent in the preparatory phase of his/her swing. However, your head should be turned toward the front wall before he/she makes contact with the ball. Not only is it dangerous to watch your opponent actually hit the ball, but the practice will slow you down in preparing for your next shot.

Etiquette

In any game that involves competition, you are encouraged to play hard in hopes of either attaining victory or having the comfort of knowing that even in defeat you gave a 100 percent effort. Sportsmanship involves the little things that go a long way in determining not only the degree of success you have but also the enjoyment you experience. Always treat your opponent with courtesy, dignity and respect. In other words, treat your opponent as you want to be treated.

1. Be prompt for your matches, which means you should be properly dressed and prepared for the warm-up routines at the scheduled time.

2. Greet your opponent and demonstrate a positive, cheerful attitude.

3. Allow your opponent a sufficient warm-up period (not to exceed five minutes) before deciding who will serve first.

4. Service can be decided by a coin toss, agreement of both players, or lagging for the short line. The latter option means that each player tries to hit a front wall shot as close as possible to the short line while standing an arm's length from the back wall. The one hitting the ball closest to the short line serves first.

5. Call out the score before each serve, giving the server's score first. In the heat of competition, the score is often temporarily forgotten. So to avoid possible confusion and/or disagreements that unnecessarily prolong the match, remember to verbalize the score after each point.

6. Conversation on the court is acceptable between points or during time-outs. To talk to yourself or your opponent during an actual rally is in poor taste and usually unnecessary. In doubles or cutthroat, it is permissible for partners to talk during the rally, using such phrases as "I have it," "Take it," etc.

7. Showing emotion during or after a rally is a natural human quality and is acceptable if done in good taste and not overdone. To hit a ball in anger, hit the wall with the racquet, or stomp around the court using vulgarity is totally unacceptable and can result in penalty points or a disqualification in tournament play.

8. Call the shots as you see them, without hesitation. If the ball skips, call it a "skip." Be fair and consistent, and realize that nobody makes 100 percent correct calls. When in doubt, ask for your opponent's opinion, or simply replay the point.

9. Regardless of the game outcome or your personal performance, be courteous after the game. Shake hands with your opponent and thank him/her for a good competitive game, a good workout, a real learning experience, or whatever you gained from the match. The key is to have something positive to say. Congratulations should always go to the winner and a word of courtesy to the loser.

2
Learning the Strokes

IMPORTANCE OF GRIP

Fundamental to success in performing the various racquetball strokes and serves is a mechanically sound grip of the racquet during the swing and contact with the ball. Utilization of a proper grip is the first step toward playing racquetball at optimum proficiency. Grip options include the Eastern forehand, Eastern backhand, Continental and Western. A player may use any number of the four grips or perform all strokes and serves with the Continental grip alone.

Quality racquetball players know that the natural "V" formed by the thumb and index finger must be properly located to get maximum results from a particular grip. The diagram on the following page indicates the specific area of the racquet where the "V" should be located to assume a desired grip. For each of the grips, the middle of the "V" should be located directly over the specified area. The proper hand position on the racquet can be likened to a handshake.

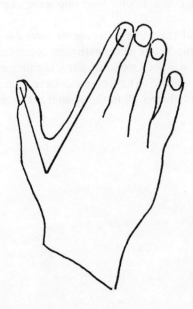

"V" formed by thumb and index finger.

10

Two other grip fundamentals should be mentioned. The racquet should be held comfortably in the hand while maneuvering on the court, with a firmer grip assumed during the backswing and especially at the moment of contact with the ball. Also, the flat end of the racquet handle and the lower part of the hand at the base of the grip should be relatively flush, as opposed to a portion of the racquet handle protruding beyond the grip of the hand or the end of the racquet being cupped inside the palm.

As their names imply, the Eastern forehand and backhand are used for hitting forehand and backhand shots, respectively. A change of grip may be made with or without the aid of the non-racquet hand. The method of changing grips is individual preference and often depends upon the amount of preparation time available for the anticipated shot.

As alluded to earlier, the Continental grip is the only type of grip that can be effective for hitting all the various racquetball shots. Maintaining the same grip for all strokes is important during fast-paced play.

Some players prefer the Western grip over the Continental or Eastern grip for hitting the forehand ceiling shot. Picking a racquet up off the floor places the hand in the correct Western grip position.

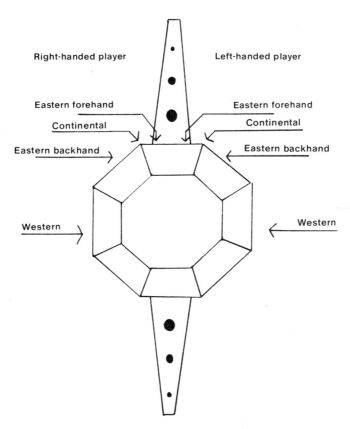

"V" location for various racquet grips.

11

SERVES

To become a versatile server, a player should learn four types of serves. The low drive power serve, half-lob (garbage), lob and Z serves are the possibilities to choose from when serving to an opponent. Lobs and half-lobs are effective only on the opponent's backhand side. The Z serve is a cross-court serve that may be hit at varying speeds but is most effective when hit at a velocity similar to the low drive power serve.

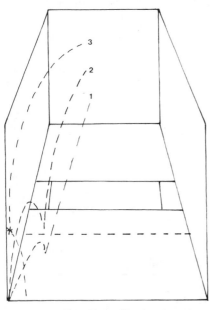

Point of aim for: (1) low drive power serve; (2) half-lob serve; (3) lob serve.

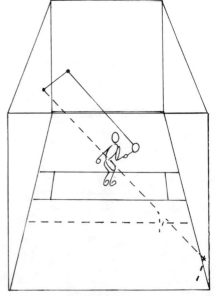

Z serve to right corner.

Instructions for serving are presented later in this chapter. Rules for serving are included in the Appendix, while service strategy is found in Chapter 5. You are advised to study the information in these sections and regularly practice the recommended stroke mechanics of the various types of serves.

OFFENSIVE SHOTS

Kill

The most potent offensive weapon in racquetball is the kill shot. The straight kill, pinch, front wall-side wall kill and overhead kill are the four types of kill shots employed in racquetball. As indicated by its name, the overhead kill is hit with an overhand motion and is a lower percentage kill shot.

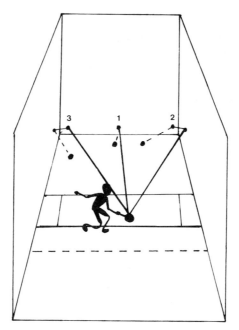

Kill shots whereby ball is contacted below knee: (1) straight; (2) pinch; (3) front wall-side wall.

Pass

Another common offensive shot in racquetball is the pass shot (cross-court and down-the-wall). Using this shot at proper times is the key to its effectiveness. The same pass shot can range from a very effective offensive play to a mere setup, depending upon the position of your opponent.

Half-Volley

Ability to hit the ball with a solid, compact stroke in fast-paced racquetball action is a valuable asset. The degree of force required to effectively hit the shot depends on the game situation. A soft shot in a corner is appropriate if your opponent is out of position in back court, but a more forceful put-away is in order when your opponent occupies center court.

Take a close look at the mechanics of the forehand and backhand strokes shown later in this chapter and visualize in your mind the action that would be required to modify the stroke into a half-volley. In other words, the half-volley backswing, stroke and follow-through are much shorter in range than the normal forehand and backhand strokes with comparatively less force applied to the ball.

13

DEFENSIVE SHOTS

Ceiling Shot

The ceiling shot is the most common defensive shot in racquetball and is routinely used by accomplished players. Commonly, the best defense against a ceiling shot is another ceiling ball; one shot tends to produce another, resulting in long, deliberate ceiling shot rallies. You must develop an adequate ceiling shot or you will forfeit many points to opponents who are proficient at hitting the shot.

Other Defensive Shots

The around-the-wall ball is a change-of-pace shot which often surprises an opponent, causing him/her to hit a weak return. This shot can be comfortably hit from the ceiling shot position or from a regular forehand position as long as the ball is struck above waist level. Once the ball drops below waist level, the around-the-wall ball becomes much more difficult to control.

Another change-of-pace defensive shot is the Z ball. The pattern of the shot resembles a high Z serve, except that the shot is hit from back court and strikes three walls.

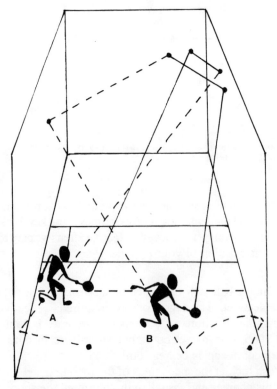

Z ball (A) and around-the-wall ball (B).

A lob shot is sometimes used as a defensive shot but must be hit with pinpoint accuracy for success. Consequently, the lob shot is a low percentage defensive shot that demonstrates limited value.

On occasion during a racquetball game, the location of the ball and the player's court position are such that he/she can effectively hit only the low percentage back-to-back wall shot. This usually happens when one player hits an elusive pass shot that can be reached by the other player but can only be hit in the direction of the back wall. Sometimes a beginner becomes infatuated with the use of this shot and uses it in situations in which another defensive shot or even an offensive shot is the proper shot selection. The back-to-back wall shot should be used only as a last resort for keeping a ball in play and thus possibly saving a point. To use the shot in any other way is poor strategy due to its low percentage effectiveness. More often than not the back-to-back wall shot results in a setup opportunity for the opponent.

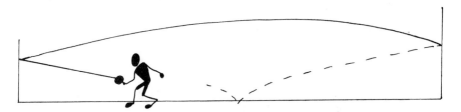

Last resort back-to-back wall shot by left-handed player.

ANALYSIS OF RACQUETBALL STROKES

Fundamentals of the low drive power serve, lob serve, back wall forehand return, forehand ceiling shot, back wall backhand return, backhand pass shot and backhand ceiling shot are pictorially presented and interpreted in this section. The use of high-speed photography offers a unique analysis of racquetball mechanics.

Low Drive Power Serve

The low drive power serve parallels the body and racquet arm action of underhand baseball pitchers. Actually, throwing underhand is the same as throwing overhand except that the players lean to their throwing side. The common deviation from the throwing motion has players approaching the boxer's uppercut punching motion. The problem is that while the punching motion is quicker in response, it cannot generate equal racquet speed.

Rear and stride legs. A short, crossover step of the rear leg behind the stride leg at the start of the power serve helps beginning players get the racquet arm back through the fully prepared position at the proper moment. However, if players get their racquet arm back appropriately, they will not lose racquet speed by not using the crossover step. The rear leg supports and propels the body forward until the stride foot contacts the floor. To maintain proper balance, a player should stride forward in a straight line. A deeply bent stride leg lowers the player to strike the ball near the floor. To avoid straining the muscles on the front (anterior) of the shoulder, the player should rotate about a single vertical axis by pushing vigorously against the stride foot.

Body. Once planted, the stride foot is the foundation for a series of body actions. First, the hips rotate forward, then snap to a stop. This initiates the forward rotation of the chest. Next, the chest snapping to a stop initiates the forward rotation of the shoulders. The shoulder snapping to a stop then initiates the forward movement of the upper arm. Finally, the upper arm snapping to a stop propels the forearm and racquet to ball contact.

To understand this concept, imagine the bullwhip action. Sequentially, the hips, chest, shoulder, upper arm and elbow imitate the bullwhip's handle. The bullwhip glides forward until the entire length of the whip is almost extended, then the heavy handle suddenly snaps to a standstill. This snapping to a standstill dramatically accelerates the tip of the whip. In the same manner, this series of body actions produces every player's maximum racquet speed.

Front arm. With the front arm holding the ball near knee level, the player should gently release the ball in front of the striding foot in order to strike the ball behind the planted stride foot (8-10 inches). After releasing the ball, the front arm bends, then reaches forward. This counterbalances the backward swing of the racquet arm. To initiate the forward drive of the racquet, the front arm pulls back to the body in a bent elbow position.

Racquet arm. With the racquet pointing generally upward and backward, the player should ease the racquet arm through the fully prepared position very early. From this moment, the racquet starts its forward drive. As the racquet starts forward, the weight of the racquet and forearm naturally coils the upper arm for its powerful inward rotation. Once the upper arm snaps to its standstill, the inward rotation of the bent elbow dramatically accelerates the racquet to ball contact. Immediately after contacting the ball, the player should raise the elbow. Otherwise, the weight of the racquet may overextend and injure the elbow.

LOW DRIVE POWER SERVE

1-1

1-2

1-3

1-4

Note that demonstrator is not wearing eye guards for photographic purposes. You are advised to always wear eye guards during play.

Photo 1-1:   Ball release and start of racquet arm's preparatory phase.
Photo 1-2:   Mid-position of stride leg.
Photo 1-3:   Start of racquet arm's forward movement.
Photo 1-4:   Stride foot fully contacting floor.

17

1-5

1-6

1-7

1-8

Photo 1-5:   Racquet upper arm parallel to floor.
Photo 1-6:   Racquet arm in proper position for explosive stroke.
Photo 1-7:   Racquet prepared to contact ball low to floor.
Photo 1-8:   Completed absorption of forward force generated by racquet arm.

Sequence photography was shot with the Canon High Speed F-1 Camera at 14 frames per second.

Photo 1-9:   Completed inward rotation of racquet elbow.
Photo 1-10:   Completed follow-through.

FURTHER ANALYSIS OF LOW DRIVE POWER SERVE

2-1   2-2

Photo 2-1:   Racquet upper arm parallel to floor.
Photo 2-2:   Racquet arm in proper position for explosive stroke.

2-3

2-4　　　　　　　　　　　　**2-5**

Photo 2-3:　Preparing for ball contact while bent-knee stride leg and bent-elbow front arm stabilize the body.

Photo 2-4:　Completed absorption of force generated by racquet arm.

Photo 2-5:　Racquet arm elbow inwardly rotating while racquet arm moves to full palm-down position.

Lob Serve

The lob serve requires a delicate touch. No aspect of this serve involves rapid movement.

Rear and stride legs. The bent rear leg supports and eases the body forward and upward until after ball contact. The stride begins at ball drop and ends just before the racquet starts forward. The stride leg does not assume body support until just before ball contact.

Body. The body remains relatively upright throughout.

Front arm and racquet arm. After releasing the ball, the front arm reaches forward, then, pulls back with little intensity. After an abbreviated backswing, the racquet arm dips below ball contact level to begin its upward and forward arc. Inward rotation of the elbow completes the lob serve. Players should avoid the common error of using a "stiff-arm" or scooping action.

LOB SERVE

3-1	3-2

Photo 3-1:   Ball release to initiate serve.
Photo 3-2:   Start of racquet arm's forward movement.

Photo 3-3:   Racquet arm prepared for controlled stroke.
Photo 3-4:   Racquet contact with ball.
Photo 3-5:   Completed absorption of force generated by racquet arm.
Photo 3-6:   Completed follow-through.

Forehand Return

Success of the forehand return depends on 1) estimating where the ball will bounce for the second time, 2) moving to that location, 3) modifying the low drive power serve mechanics and 4) striking the ball close to the floor. To modify the low drive power serve mechanics, the player should decrease the hip and chest rotation, abbreviate the shoulder movement and accentuate the upper arm and elbow inward rotation. Whenever possible, the player should allow the ball to rebound off the back wall. In the back wall backhand return, players should position themselves closer to the rear wall than the second bounce location and strike the ball behind the planted stride foot while moving forward. Turning the head and upper body to almost face the back wall facilitates this stroke.

FOREHAND RETURN

4-1   4-2

Photo 4-1:   Start of racquet arm's forward movement.
Photo 4-2:   Racquet upper arm parallel to floor.

Photo 4-3:   Racquet arm fully cocked for explosive stroke.
Photo 4-4:   Immediately before racquet contact with ball.
Photo 4-5:   Completed absorption of force generated by racquet arm and completed inward rotation of elbow.
Photo 4-6:   Completed follow-through.

Forehand Ceiling Shot

As in the lob serve, no aspect of the forehand ceiling shot involves rapid movement. Players should abbreviate the overhand throwing motion primarily with inward rotation of the elbow.

FOREHAND CEILING SHOT

5-1

5-2

5-3

Photo 5-1: Start of racquet arm's forward movement.
Photo 5-2: Immediately before racquet contact with ball.
Photo 5-3: Completed follow-through.

Backhand Return

Success of the backhand return depends on 1) estimating where the ball will bounce for a second time, 2) moving to that location and 3) striking the ball close to the floor. Whenever possible, a player should allow the ball to rebound off the back wall. In the back wall backhand return, players should position themselves closer to the rear wall than the second bounce location and strike the ball behind the planted stride foot while moving forward. Turning the head and upper body to almost face the back wall facilitates this stroke.

Rear and stride legs. The rear leg supports and propels the body forward until the stride leg contacts the floor. To maintain proper balance, the player should stride forward in a straight line. A deeply bent stride leg lowers the player to strike the ball near the floor. To avoid straining the muscles on the back (posterior) of the shoulder, the player should rotate about a single vertical axis by pushing vigorously against the stride foot.

Body. Once planted, the stride foot is the foundation for a series of body actions. First, the hips rotate forward, then snap to a stop. This initiates the forward rotation of the chest. Next, the chest snapping to a stop initiates the forward rotation of the shoulders. However, the shoulder snap does not initiate the forward movement of the upper arm. Rather, the shoulder and upper arm function as one at a fixed 90° angle. Finally, the combined shoulder and upper arm snapping to a stop propels the forearm and racquet to ball contact.

Rear arm. The rear arm of the backhand stroke counterbalances the racquet arm. The rear arm should begin its backward motion at the same time as the racquet arm begins its forward drive.

Racquet arm. With the racquet pointing generally backward and upward, a player should ease the racquet arm through the fully prepared position very early. From this moment, the racquet starts its forward drive. Once the upper arm snaps to a standstill, the outward rotation of the bent elbow dramatically accelerates the racquet to ball contact. As soon as possible after contacting the ball, a player should lower the elbow. Otherwise, the weight of the racquet may overextend and injure the elbow.

BACKHAND RETURN

Photo sequence reads right to left for the backhand.

6-2   6-1

6-4   6-3

Photo 6-1: Completion of rear leg adjustment to ball's location.
Photo 6-2: Start of racquet's forward movement.
Photo 6-3: Stride foot fully contacting floor.
Photo 6-4: Racquet upper arm parallel to floor.

Photo 6-5:   Racquet arm fully cocked for explosive stroke.
Photo 6-6:   Immediately before racquet contact with ball.
Photo 6-7:   Completed absorption of force generated by racquet arm.
Photo 6-8:   Completed follow-through.

Front Wall Backhand Pass

In the front wall backhand pass, the player strikes the ball either in the air or on the first bounce. Success of this stroke depends on 1) moving to the proper location and 2) modifying the mechanics of the backhand return. To modify the mechanics of the backhand return, the player should decrease the hip and chest rotation, abbreviate the shoulder and upper arm movement and accentuate the elbow outward rotation.

FRONT WALL BACKHAND PASS

Photo sequence reads right to left for the backhand.

7-2   7-1

Photo 7-1:   Start of racquet arm's forward movement.
Photo 7-2:   Racquet upper arm parallel to floor.

7-4   **7-3**

7-6   **7-5**

Photo 7-3: Racquet arm fully cocked for explosive stroke.
Photo 7-4: Immediately before racquet contact with ball.
Photo 7-5: Completed absorption of force generated by racquet arm.
Photo 7-6: Completed follow-through.

8-1

8-2

Photo 8-1: Racquet upper arm parallel to floor.
Photo 8-2: Racquet arm fully cocked for explosive stroke.

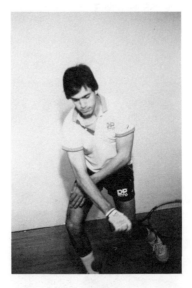

8-4

Photo 8-3: Immediately before racquet contact with ball.
Photo 8-4: Completed absorption of force generated by racquet arm.

Backhand Ceiling Shot

As in the forehand ceiling shot, no aspect of the backhand ceiling shot involves rapid movement. The player should abbreviate the backhand pass mechanics primarily with outward rotation of the elbow.

BACKHAND CEILING SHOT

Photo sequence reads right to left for the backhand.

9-2   9-1

Photo 9-1:   **Start of racquet arm's preparatory phase.**
Photo 9-2:   **Start of racquet arm's forward movement.**

9-4   **9-3**

9-6   **9-5**

Photo 9-3: Racquet upper arm and forearm parallel to floor.
Photo 9-4: Racquet contact with ball.
Photo 9-5: Completed absorption of force generated by racquet arm.
Photo 9-6: Completed follow-through.

3

Improving Your Skills

Quality racquetball play requires a high degree of neuromuscular skill, involving such physical skills as coordination, quickness, agility and endurance. Practice is a necessity for a player to significantly improve his/her skill level. The old adage, "Practice makes perfect," will never be true for the sport of racquetball, but it illustrates the importance of practice. Most serious racquetball players, especially the professionals, spend as much, if not more, time practicing, as they do playing competitively.

Stroke repetition and drill work in practice sessions must be systematic and progressive to be effective. Plan your practice sessions with some objectives in mind, and do not spend time on advanced strokes until you can perform the basic forehand and backhand strokes with some degree of confidence and skill. Proficiency at hitting the kill shot, for example, is more easily attained once a player has some control of shot velocity and placement on the basic forehand and backhand strokes.

No magic formula exists to improve a player's game or promote his/her progression from a beginner to an advanced player. Only through regular practice, hard work and concentration during play can you expect to progress in skill development. Improvement builds confidence; thus practice tends to improve the mental component of a player's game as well as the physical.

Remember that skills progression takes time. Be patient, and give yourself a chance to get better at your own pace. Avoid comparing your progress with that of other players. Be assured that serious attention to practice and a good mental attitude is a combination that will eventually work for you in your effort to improve.

Practice drills may involve only one person, and certain drills are designed for two or more players. Individual and group drills are equally significant, but the most important thing to remember is to start with the drills that are consistent with your current skill level and progress from that point at your own rate. Once a drill has been mastered, move on to the next drill. Remember that accuracy and consistency are much more important objectives than trying to overpower the ball. Work on placement first, then develop power once you have the confidence.

Individual drills are presented first, starting with the basic beginning drills.

FOREHAND STROKE DRILL

Objective:

To improve your ability to control ball placement when performing the forehand stroke.

35

Description:

Stand at the service line three to five feet from the side wall on your forehand side. Point your toes directly toward the side wall. Assume a ready position with the racquet, and hold the ball in your non-racquet hand. Drop the ball to the side and slightly in front of your body. Step into the ball, and bend your knees as you hit the ball with a flat racquet face. Try to make the ball rebound back to you on a straight-line path close to the side wall. Stop the ball, and repeat the action until the desired consistency has been achieved.

General Comments:

Start this drill while standing in an erect position. As you drop the ball, bend your legs. The leg action is vital in this drill, as it is in the execution of most racquetball shots.

Do not drop the ball too close to your body. If you do, you will not be able to control the placement of the ball. After practicing from this position, repeat the action while positioned at the short line. Eventually move back to within three feet of the back wall and repeat the drill.

BACKHAND STROKE DRILL

Objective:

To improve your ability to control ball placement when performing the backhand stroke. The backhand stroke is unnatural for the average beginner, which makes this drill especially important. For relative improvement, the backhand stroke must be practiced more than the forehand.

Description:

Stand at the service line three to five feet from the side wall on your backhand side. At the beginning of the drill, the non-racquet hand should be located underneath the racquet to lift your racquet high at the start of the stroke. The backhand stroke should be repeated at progressively greater distances, as in the forehand stroke drill.

General Comments:

Drop the ball at a distance, so you are forced to step toward the ball with your right foot as you hit the shot. This action provides you more power in hitting the ball. Also, drop the ball well in front of you, so you are positioned somewhat behind the ball when contact is made.

RALLY DRILL

Objective:

To improve your timing, judgment and racquet control.

Description:

This drill involves hitting the ball continuously after it bounces against the front wall (with or without striking the side wall) with the forehand and backhand. To start, assume a position in the center of the court behind the short line. Then bounce the ball waist high and hit it to the front wall. As the ball rebounds from the front wall, let it bounce, and move into correct position to hit it again. As long as the ball is in play, keep returning it to the front wall. Remember to stay behind the short line and hit the ball after it bounces one time.

General Comments:

First, rally the ball with the forehand and then the backhand, contacting the front wall only. As you develop more skill, alternate the strokes and gradually move closer to the front wall. This will increase the tempo of play. You should also vary the speed and direction of the ball as well as your position on the court. These variations will make the drill gamelike.

VOLLEY DRILL

Objective:

To develop your reflex action and hand-eye coordination.

Description:

This drill is similar in description and execution to the rally drill except that you hit the ball continuously on the fly after it rebounds from the front wall, and continue to return the ball to the front wall in this manner as long as possible.

General Comments:

Volley first with the forehand and then with the backhand, contacting the front wall only. As your skill increases, alternate the strokes and gradually move closer to the front wall. This will increase the tempo of the drill and sharpen your reflex action.

CROSS-COURT SHOT DRILL

Objective:

To learn to control the angle on cross-court pass shots.

Description:

This drill can be used to practice with either the forehand or backhand. Similar in description and execution to the forehand stroke drill, the cross-court shot drill involves striking the ball in such a manner that it will hit the front wall at an angle and travel cross-court without hitting the wall on the opposite side.

General Comments:

Initially execute this shot near the front wall with first the forehand and then the backhand. As your skill increases, gradually move deeper in the court. Watch closely the angle the ball must take to make the pass shots successful. Be sure to practice these shots on both the forehand and backhand side.

BACK WALL FOREHAND DRILL

Objective:

To develop your skill in hitting forehand shots off the back wall.

Description:

Take a position approximately five feet away from the back wall. Stand six feet away from the forehand side wall, with the toes pointing directly toward the side wall. With your free hand, toss the ball at medium speed off the back wall at waist level. The ball should rebound off the back wall and bounce slightly in front of you and to the side. As the ball moves out and away from you, shuffle your feet until the ball drops below your waist. Allow the ball to drop at knee level and then strike it, using a regular forehand sidearm stroke. Hit the ball off the front wall at an angle slightly to the right of your body, so that it rebounds on a line to your hitting side.

General Comments:

Keep your eye on the ball at all times. Practice lateral shuffling of the feet, not running, since turning to run with the shot will cause your body to automatically rotate away from the ball and will hinder your ability to perform the stroke properly.

Toss the ball off the back wall in such a manner that you allow sufficient room to step into the shot and thus hit the ball with force.

BACK WALL BACKHAND DRILL

Objective:

This drill will help prepare you for returning back wall shots or serves to your backhand.

Description:

Assume a position five feet away from the back wall. Face the side wall on your backhand side, standing six feet away. Again point the toes toward the side wall. With your non-racquet hand, toss the ball off the back wall at waist level. Throw the ball slightly away from yourself to allow room for your stroke. Allow the ball to bounce slightly past you as you shuffle into hitting position. Step into the shot, contacting the ball at knee level or below. Stroke the ball into the front wall so that it rebounds on a line through the hitting area.

General Comments:

Let the ball get out in front of you before making contact. Shuffle along with the ball until it reaches knee level. You will have to wait for what seems like a long time before stepping into the shot and hitting it to the front wall. Be sure to take a full swing at the ball, not punch at it with a half-swing as beginners often do.

FOREHAND CEILING DRILL

Objective:

To develop your ability to hit a ceiling shot from deep back court.

Description:

Stand an arm and racquet's length from the back wall, facing the side wall on the forehand side. Bounce the ball near your front foot, then step into the ball and strike it with an underhand motion to the ceiling first. Aim the ball three feet away from the front wall. The ball should definitely contact the ceiling first, then rebound into the back court. You should be waiting to hit another ceiling ball, only this time perform the shot with the usual overhand motion. After initiating the overhand swinging motion, step forward and contact the ball as your arm is fully extending above your head, again sending the ball back to the ceiling. This motion is similar to the throwing motion.

General Comments:

Try to hit consecutive overhead ceiling shots to approximately the same location. When you miss a shot or the ball gets out of control, start the drill again with the underhand motion.

BACKHAND CEILING DRILL

Objective:

To develop your ability to hit a backhand ceiling shot during rallies and on service returns.

Description:

Stand on the backhand side an arm and racquet's length from the back wall, facing the side wall. Start the drill by bouncing the ball out in front of you. Then step into the shot and contact the ball with an underhand motion, driving the ball to the ceiling first, about three feet from the front wall. Follow through in an upward motion toward the ceiling with a full swing. As the ball rebounds off the ceiling, remain facing the side wall. Unlike in the forehand ceiling shot, your body should not face the front wall. Swing the backhand arm out away from your body and upward, so that you meet the ball off the front foot above head level. Continue to strike the ball to the ceiling first, using the same target as before.

General Comments:

Keep your feet pointing to the backhand side wall through the entire stroke. This will enable you to maintain good balance and to develop consistency in performing the backhand ceiling shot. This is a very difficult shot to master, so do not become discouraged if your accuracy or consistency is poor at the outset.

KILL SHOT DRILL

Objective:

To develop proficiency in hitting a straight or corner kill shot, with either the forehand or backhand.

Description:

Position yourself just behind the short line about three feet away from the forehand side wall or backhand side wall. You are advised to practice the forehand kill first. With the free hand, toss the ball up and out in front of you so that you will have room to step into the ball. As the ball bounces, lower your racquet and get your legs positioned to hit it on its downward flight. Contact should be made at or below knee level, and the ball should be driven straight into the front wall as low as possible. Stay down on the ball and maintain a low, level swing. A straight kill contacts the front wall about two to six inches above the floor and does not hit a side wall. A corner pinch kill involves the same swinging motion, only the point of aim is such that the ball contacts the side wall first. The initial point of contact should be two to six inches above the floor, approximately one foot away from the front wall.

The other corner kill shot, the front wall-side wall kill, is executed in the same manner, except that the ball hits the front wall first.

General Comments:

Keep your eyes on the ball and do not overswing. A successful kill shot depends more on accuracy than power or speed. Be patient and wait until the ball has dropped below the knee before making contact. Timing is a very important element in learning the kill shot.

SIDE WALL DRILL

Objective:

To become proficient at hitting balls that carom off or hug the side walls.

Description:

Stand even with the short line and an arm and racquet's length from the side wall. Touch the side wall with the racquet so that you have established the fact that you are in the proper position. Hold the ball in your non-racquet hand, and toss the ball high but lightly, so it gently touches the side wall. As the ball comes down off the side wall, move away using a shuffling motion, attempting to stay in a proper hitting position with the ball being played off your front foot. Allow the ball to reach at least knee level, then hit either a down-the-wall pass, cross-court pass, pinch or straight kill.

General Comments:

This drill can be done from the front court or back court and should be attempted from both the forehand and backhand side. On

40

the down-the-wall pass and straight kill, allow the ball to rebound away from the wall one to two feet initially, then take aim closer to the wall until the ball actually hugs the wall on the carom. Remember to contact the ball at knee level or below.

Partner drills (drills involving two players) are also valuable in practicing racquetball skills. They are especially effective when two players of near equal ability are assigned as partners. The following are four examples of this type of drill.

SERVE AND RETURN DRILL

Objective:

> To increase your proficiency in executing the various serves and return of serve.

Description:

> One person stands in the service zone and the other in the receiving area. The server executes a particular service while the receiver attempts to complete a successful return.

General Comments:

> The server should start with the basic serves and practice each one twenty times, ten to the forehand and ten to the backhand side. The receiver should attempt to return the ball as if in actual competition. Once the receiver completes a return, the drill is then repeated. In a beginner class, it is a good idea for the server to call out the type of upcoming serve so the receiver can have a moment to think about the type of return he/she will attempt.

CROSS-COURT RALLY DRILL

Objective:

> To give you more confidence at hitting mid-court shots when the ball is rebounding to you quickly.

Description:

> Stand in the service zone and face the forehand side wall while standing about three feet away. Your opponent should also stand three feet into the service zone and face the wall on the backhand side. Initiate a rally by driving the ball at knee level into the front wall first, so that it rebounds straight out to your opponent's backhand. Your opponent then should try to hit the ball back to your forehand side. This sequence continues until one of you fails to return the ball, or until the ball goes out of control.

General Comments:

> The drill can be done exclusively on one side. Practice forehand-to-forehand or backhand-to-backhand. At first, limit play to the front wall, but later you should include the side and back walls in the drill.

SETUP AND SHOOT DRILL

Objective:

To increase your proficiency in executing various shots under gamelike conditions.

Description:

This is a method of practicing the various racquetball shots with another player. One player stands in the service area and hits the ball, trying to set up his/her partner for a particular shot. At a position five feet behind the short line, the other player then must maneuver to execute one of the common shots in racquetball. The player's shot selection is dependent upon the type of setup provided.

General Comments:

During your turn at returning a setup, have a particular shot in mind when getting into position to hit the ball. Practice a particular shot until some degree of skill is attained. To help in this regard, the player starting the action should call out the shot intended.

FOOTWORK DRILLS

Footwork drills include the side-shuffle, crossover step, oblique angle running and the combination drill. These are useful as individual or partner drills.

Objective:

To improve your proficiency in setting up to execute a particular shot.

Description:

The side-shuffle movement is similar to that used in basketball. It is a series of quick lateral movements. The crossover step is used to hit a ball that rebounds near either side of a player. When executing this step, you should pivot on the foot nearest the ball and swing the other foot in front of the body toward the direction of the oncoming ball. Oblique running is a pattern of running that takes place during a game. It usually occurs when a player runs to hit the ball in either corner of the court. The combination drill is a drill that combines all the previous footwork drills into one routine. To practice this drill independently, you should stand in the service area and hit a half-lob serve so that it will bounce off the back wall. After serving, retreat immediately to the back court and return the ball to the front wall. In other words you are returning your own serve.

The doubles drill is also initiated with a service. The other player stands in the service area away from the server. Once the serve is hit, the player responsible for returning the ball should run to back court and get into position to make the return. Correct body positioning should take priority over shot placement in this practice drill.

General Comments:

At first, practice these drills independently, then employ them as partner drills. During a combination drill, you should start in the center court position, then shuffle a few feet to one side and stop, then hit the imaginary ball and return to the center court position. Next you run obliquely to one of the corners of the court, hit the ball and then return to the original position. Keep on doing this until you complete the whole cycle, i.e., touching both side walls and all four corners of the court. We recommend that you practice the forehand side first, then work on the backhand side.

4

Developing Court Sense

Racquetball is more than a game of physical skill. It is a test of wits, concentration and stamina. These factors often have a greater bearing on the outcome of a match than the ability level of the opponents. Progression in the development of court sense is as important as mastering a crack serve or deadly kill shot. Playing a "smart" game can sometimes nullify the edge an opponent may have in stroke proficiency. By applying the information contained in this chapter, you will be able to play a more intelligent game of racquetball.

COURT POSITION AND COVERAGE

Advantage Position

An area starting about two feet behind the short line and extending toward the back wall at dimensions of approximately ten by sixteen feet is known as the "center court" area, even though the location of the area is not the center of the court per se. A more descriptive term might be the "advantage" position or "percentage" position because most of the game is played in that area, and it is the area of the court from where the offensive kill and pass shots are best executed. Jockeying for position in center court is a way of life for the experienced player and must become ingrained in your mental approach to the game if you are to ever perform at a maximum level.

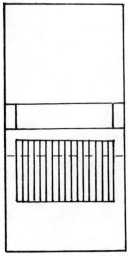

Center court or advantage area.

44

Center Court Philosophy

The essence of racquetball is to drive the opponent out of the center court area as much as possible with well-executed shots. Once this happens, the opponent is on the defensive and is more likely to hit a lower percentage shot than desired. This will allow you to move into a position of advantage, ready to hit a high percentage shot should your opponent's shot come into the center court area.

Competing for Center Court Position

Your ability to execute shots that force the opponent out of the center court area is truly the key to gaining an advantage in the center court game. Another effective tactic in helping to attain an edge in this important aspect of game strategy can be used when both you and your opponent are positioned in center court. The ploy is to relinquish court space grudgingly for your opponent to hit a shot. Sufficient room to hit the ball should be permitted and no more. You should stay as close as possible to the middle of the advantage area without hindering your opponent's shot or path of movement. It is important to remember that allowing an opponent the length of one additional step is crucial, since the typical racquetball game produces numerous situations whereby shots barely evade the reach of players.

Energy Conservation

Success in implementing the center court strategy conserves a player's energy. In general, a player who fails to return to the center court position after a shot must in one burst of energy move a greater distance to retrieve balls than the player who regularly returns to the center court area. Over the run of a match, this shortcoming takes its toll in missed opportunities, lost points and wasted energy. If you minimize the importance of this flaw, you will never reach your racquetball potential.

Principles of Court Coverage

A prompt return to center court between shots is undoubtedly the major principle of court coverage. Learning to anticipate your opponent's next move or type of shot is also fundamental to good court coverage. Sometimes an extra split-second gained in moving to the ball means the difference between scoring or losing serve, or, on the other hand, breaking your opponent's serve or losing a point. Getting into the habit of watching your opponent set up for a shot is one way to become proficient at court coverage. Many players reveal the type of shot they are preparing to make, which is advantageous to the opposition in preparing to take the next shot in the rally. You should watch the opponent until a split-second before contact is made, then face the front wall in a ready position for hitting the next shot. This action will enable you to react more quickly and effectively to the eventual shot taken while at the same time avoiding the possibility of an eye injury caused by the moving ball.

Setting up with the knees bent and the racquet held at waist level is a fundamentally sound practice when preparing for the next required movement in competition. In addition, taking a center court position two to three feet in back court as opposed to straddling the short line (exact middle court) is suggested, since the typical racquetball player can move forward much more quickly than backward.

Center court or advantage position.

SHOT SELECTION AND PLACEMENT

As emphasized previously, the basic strategy in racquetball is to hit shots that force the opponent out of the middle of the court. Running the opponent left and right, and up and back, until a shot either eludes him/her or causes a weak return is the object of the game. A tendency on your part to hit shots that wind up in mid-court will give your opponent an advantage that is difficult to overcome and must be avoided. You must remember that the kill and pass shots are more easily executed from the center court position than elsewhere on the court.

Point of Ball Contact

Point of contact with the ball is extremely important in the game of racquetball. One of the most difficult concepts to instill in a beginner is the idea that ball contact should be made between the ankle and knee whenever feasible. Underhanded shots demonstrate higher percentage for scoring and breaking serve. However, beginning racquetball players in the United States invariably overuse the overhand and sidearm motion in striking the ball, due in large degree to their exposure to such sports as baseball, softball, football, basketball and tennis.

Reading Wall Caroms

Behind the recommendation to contact the ball low on offensive shots is the basic law of mechanics, "The angle of incidence equals the angle of reflection." This means that, exclusive of wall friction and ball spin, a racquetball caroms off a wall at the same angle it strikes the wall. On a percentage basis, balls struck at waist level are much more easily retrieved than those contacted between the knee and ankle. You will never play at a maximum level without understanding and employing this concept. If a veteran player were to enumerate the cardinal principles of racquetball, the practice of allowing the ball to drop low to the floor before making contact would be at or near the top of the list.

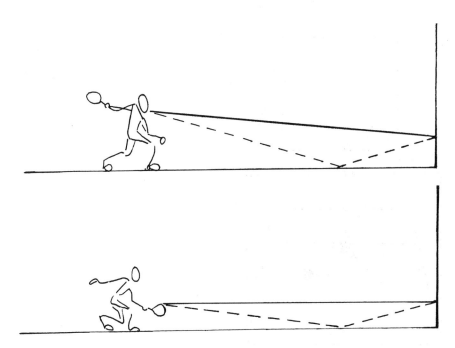

Rebound angle equals angle of contact.

Favoring the Forehand

Since virtually all racquetball players, regardless of ability level, possess a stronger forehand than backhand, many experienced performers advise the developing player to favor the forehand over the backhand when hitting a ball from the middle of the court or from an area that shades the backhand side. This recommendation is based on the assumption that the player has proper time to comfortably set up for the shot. The possibility of losing good court position when setting up for the opponent's next shot is a risk that you must take when moving into backhand territory to use the forehand. You must determine whether the forehand opportunity is worth the step or two lost in returning to proper court position.

Tips for Beginners and Intermediate Players

Staying in the center court area and hitting to the corners or down the side walls is the secret to keeping the opponent away from center court and in a defensive posture. This philosophy should dominate your game, so that the habit of moving the opponent around on the court becomes a natural thing to do when in competition. However, you should realize that many of your shots will angle toward center court due to poor shot placement caused by hitting high shots off the side wall. Remember that patience and avoidance of discouragement are needed in the learning process.

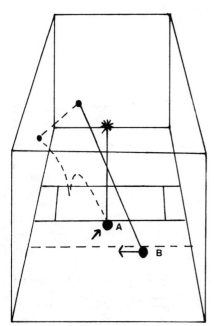

Player A kills player B's setup.

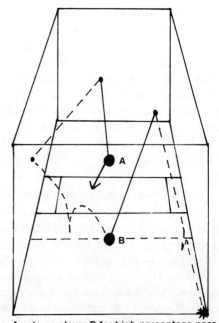

Player A sets up player B for high percentage pass shot.

Intermediate players can be more selective than beginners in taking shots, favoring high percentage shots according to individual skill. On setups in the middle of the court, the experienced player's best shot is the kill, except when the opponent is in front court. In that case, the pass is the highest percentage shot. Beginners should also try to hit a type of kill shot on setups, for two reasons. First, the concentration required to hit a kill shot helps the novice develop the habit of allowing the ball to drop low to the floor before making contact. Second, the beginner will never advance out of that ability category until at least an adequate kill shot is learned.

General Tips on Front Court Shot Selection

The type of shot used by a player is influenced by his/her court position as well as the opponent's. When you are in front court, an offensive shot is your best choice, regardless of your opponent's position. In addition to the pass, the soft (drop) shot in the corners is an effective shot to use in this situation, especially if your opponent is positioned at mid-court or beyond. The kill (straight, pinch or front wall-side wall) is effective if your opponent is in back court but should be avoided when both you and your opponent are in front court. The pass is then the clear choice.

General Tips on Mid-Court Shot Selection

Mid-court shot selection also depends on your opponent's court position and is affected by the particular circumstance in the center court game at the time of the shot. For example, one step can mean the difference between the extremes of having time for a corner kill shot or being forced to either flick the ball back weakly to the front wall or hit the equally low percentage back-to-back wall shot. You have a wide variety of high percentage shots available to you when positioned in center court. The key is to choose the one that has the best chance of eluding your opponent. A kill shot is not recommended when your opponent is in the forecourt, and neither is a pass if he/she is in back court.

General Tips on Back Court Shot Selection

In back court, defensive shots are usually in order because you are out of offensive shot range and must avoid setting up your opponent with shots that rebound toward the middle of the court. Ceiling balls, Z balls and around-the-wall shots are commonly used when players are positioned within eight feet of the back wall. However, in a situation where your opponent is also positioned in back court, a type of kill or overhead shot can be effective. Conversely, a kill is a poor choice when your opponent is in front court.

Playing Potential Volleys

Air balls that are approaching you at a level below the waist when you are in mid-court must be played, while those passing above your waist should be allowed to hit the back wall for a higher percentage shot opportunity. Balls passing below your waist in mid-court will generally die in the back court before you can retreat and retrieve them.

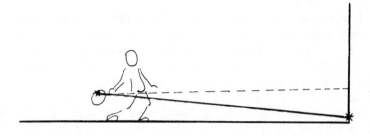

Ball approaches player below waist level; player kills ball in right corner.

Ball approaches player above waist level; player allows ball to pass, then retreats to back court to set up for forehand shot.

Reading the Front Wall

Proficiency at reading the front wall should be a priority objective. Caroms a foot or less from the floor must be returned as well as possible under the circumstances. Such rebounds are usually kill shots and are often moving rapidly. Balls hitting the front wall between one and two feet from the floor should be cut off in mid-court, generally with a kill or pass shot. Rebounds between two and four feet can sometimes be volleyed, but this depends on the speed of the carom. Balls leaving the wall at four feet or higher will almost always reach the back wall and should be allowed to do so before a return shot is hit.

Awareness of Scoring Range and Shot Potential

Knowledge of scoring range is essential to reach a quality performance level in racquetball. Kill and pass shots are excellent shot selections in high percentage situations but become much lower percentage shots when taken from deep back court. Pinch shots from the back quarter of the court are also placed in the low percentage category and should never be attempted from the back wall. Diagonal kill shots should be avoided because their execution requires near-perfect placement. Even small errors in placement can result in the ball hitting short of the front wall or too high on the wall, resulting in a setup for your opponent in mid-court. Around-the-wall balls and the Z ball often end up in the middle of the court but can be useful as defensive shots in certain situations. They are especially effective for changing the pace of a game or for surprising the opponent at times when more conventional shots are anticipated.

When you are positioned in deep back court, your best weapon is the ceiling shot. Skill at hitting this shot will aid you greatly in regaining the center court position. Players often score or break serve with ceiling shots that die in back wall corners, particularly those hit to the backhand side. However, an offensive shot is advised over the ceiling shot whenever feasible. Ceiling shots simply do not possess the offensive potential of a kill or pass shot.

Using the Overhead Shot

Your shot arsenal will be more potent if it contains an overhead shot. In a ceiling shot rally, one player may become too relaxed near the back wall, increasing the potential for a successful overhead shot by the other. The overhead is reasonably easy to camouflage, as the hitting motion closely resembles that of a ceiling shot. Even a mediocre overhead shot will sometimes catch by surprise and evade the opponent who becomes too complacent in the ceiling ball competition. Aim the ball low and toward one of the corners.

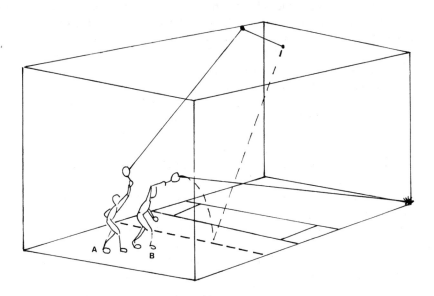

Player B ends ceiling ball rally with overhead kill.

Flexibility in Shot Selection and Placement

One thing you must always guard against is becoming predictable in shot selection and placement. The intelligent opponent will take advantage of this error in habit by assuming a court position conducive to hitting high percentage shots. Employing an assortment of shots and using both sides of the front wall for pass, pinch and ceiling shots negates any advantage your opponent may gain from overplaying certain areas of the court. Actually, overplaying a particular court area can become a liability when competing against a player who mixes his/her shots well.

Shot Velocity

Generally, shots of high velocity are more effective than softer shots. A bad habit to get into is to overuse the soft shot component of your game. The smart opponent will quickly get wise to this tactic and edge toward the front wall in anticipation of the soft shot. He/she is then in a favorable position to hit successful pinch, pass and kill shots from the forecourt.

MENTAL ATTITUDE AND STYLE OF PLAY

There is a definite "mind game" played in racquetball, along with the matching of physical skill. Your progress in the mental approach to the game should be commensurate to your physical skill development. Superiority in court savvy is the deciding factor in many racquetball matches.

Importance of Concentration

Discipline and patience characterize the smart racquetball player. Learning to concentrate on the court is the first basic step toward acquiring these competitive traits. As simple as it may seem, the development of concentration skills must be worked at with the same degree of intensity and diligence as that required for advancement in stroke proficiency.

The player with good concentration skills can take advantage of an opponent who overuses a particular shot or is predictable in shot placement. Returning to center court whenever feasible is a natural tendency of this type of player. When positioned in the center court area, the alert player more commonly follows the principle of volleying balls hit on a line below waist level and retreating to hit them off the back wall when they are passing at a level above the waist. When jockeying for center court position, this player habitually stays as close as possible to the opponent without committing a hinder. Additionally, the player who has developed a power of concentration on the court constantly looks to score or break serve but passes up a low percentage opportunity with a defensive shot that may improve his/her chances on the next opportunity. Watching opponents during their shot preparation in case they show a weakness in disguising shot selection is another good habit of the player who exhibits the ability to concentrate. The thinking player also learned early in his/her development the importance of making contact with the ball as close to ankle level as possible on most shots, as well as the value of being in a ready position as often as possible throughout the course of a game.

PERCENTAGE RACQUETBALL

Definition of Percentage Racquetball

By now you are probably aware that the foregoing paragraphs have described what some racquetball followers call "percentage racquetball." Playing percentage racquetball is the recommended way to get maximum effectiveness from your game. To play percentage racquetball simply means to consistently employ the shots and tactics that your experience has shown to be effective in the particular game situation. In other words, the odds for success should be considered in every game circumstance. Every aspect of the game should be calculated, some things before the match and others during competition.

Your first impression may be that holding too close to the philosophy of percentage racquetball could make you too predictable, thus becoming a liability to your game instead of an asset. To allay any possible skepticism, you are reminded that percentage racquetball does not mean that the pass shot, for example, is always hit on one side of the front wall, or that you should not alternate front wall corners on pinch shot placement. There are situations when you and your opponent will know which shot should be taken, yet that particular shot is the best selection if executed properly. In many instances during game play, a well-executed shot will lead to a score or service break, even though your opponent defends the shot as well as possible. Often, there simply is no effective defense for a well-placed offensive shot.

You are further reminded that many decisions made during game play other than shot selection and placement comprise the percentage racquetball approach to playing the game. Discipline in assuming court position for the particular shot being defended is as much a part of the percentage game as the right choice in shot selection. Maintaining concentration on overall game strategy is another important element in attaining proficiency at playing the percentage game.

No two racquetball performers are exactly alike in playing ability and style. Each player's collective strengths and weaknesses are unique to him/her. Your understanding of this important concept will enable you to progress more rapidly than one who uses the same strategy against all opponents. Supporters of the percentage game study each opponent's playing style, analyzing each aspect of his/her play to determine strong features and shortcomings. Sometimes several matches may be required for you to complete a thorough investigation of an opponent, but thereafter you can routinely follow a particular game plan until further revisions are needed.

Percentage Racquetball and Player's Physical Condition

Two factors players sometimes overlook that have a direct bearing on the percentage game are the pre-match warm-up and physical conditioning of the player. Pre-match warm-up is necessary to prepare the body physiologically for competition. It is also a time that you should use to prepare yourself mentally and psychologically for the task at hand. Lack of attention to warm-up may give your opponent an undue advantage in the percentage game.

To reach maximum potential in racquetball, a player must be in good physical condition. The serious student of racquetball will complement his/her racquetball playing with a physical conditioning program. Player stamina or endurance is of paramount importance in closely contested matches. The player slowest to fatigue in the third game throws the odds in his/her favor. Thus, proponents of the percentage game recognize the importance of staying in good physical condition.

5

Learning Game Strategy

Proficiency in implementing effective game strategy is imperative if you are to play quality racquetball. To more thoroughly understand principles of strategy and to maximize your potential for putting these principles into practice, you are advised to give equal attention to learning the rules of racquetball presented in the Appendix.

SERVICE STRATEGY

Server Position

Advocates of the percentage game serve in the center area of the service zone. This is true for players who serve with a crossover step or for those who use the one-step approach when serving. Consistency in service placement will be attained much more quickly and easily if you uniformly serve from the middle of the service zone. You do not have to constantly recalculate the speed of the serve and the point of aim on the front wall. Becoming consistent in service placement is difficult enough even for players who consistently serve from the same location, since a ball striking the front wall only a few inches off the desired point of aim can mean the difference between an effective serve or an easy setup for an opponent. Balls ricocheting to mid-court because of poor service placement will force you out of an advantage position and minimize your chances of getting another shot in the rally.

Player A's point of aim for serving: (1) low drive power serve; (2) half-lob; (3) lob.

Beginners have a bad habit of serving while positioned several steps away from the middle of the service zone. Aside from hindering their consistency in service placement, this practice causes them to forfeit the advantage position in center court. Although the server is only a few steps away from the ideal service location, the time required to move back to center court is precious time lost in reacting to the opponent's service return. Furthermore, the quick retreat to center court after the serve leaves a player vulnerable to a return directed behind him/her. In other words, taking a position too far to the left or right of center court when you are serving can place you at a disadvantage in hitting the next shot, regardless of which side your opponent may return the serve. The thinking is that a player can move right or left from center court more rapidly and effectively than one can move from one of the service box sides to the other side of the court, or in that direction, and then have to quickly go back toward the side vacated. The player who persists in serving from an extreme position in the service zone is violating an important principle of percentage racquetball.

Serving Motion

Crafty servers disguise the type of serve intended by using the same preliminary motion for all serves. Until contact is made with the ball, the opponent should not be able to detect what type of serve to expect. By this time, the deception may have already paid dividends, as the opponent may have misguessed the type of serve coming and, as a result, be placed at a distinct disadvantage in attempting to return the serve. Players will commonly sacrifice the opportunity to conceal a lob serve to ensure better control of that soft type of serve. But some players do effectively combine deception and quality in performing all types of serves. This is an important point for you to remember when performing the serve.

Immediate Position After Service

Once the serve is completed, you should retreat to a position about three feet or so behind the short line to await the return. From this position, you can select from a variety of percentage shots. Watch your opponent prepare to return the ball, in case any telltale signs emerge as to the type of return planned. It is sometimes wise to shade one side of the center court position, either to favor the forehand side to some degree or to hedge against a player who overuses one side of the court in returning serves. Remember that slowness in leaving the service zone can make you a victim of pass shots, or you may be handcuffed by the low drive shots that land at your feet.

In preparation for hitting your opponent's return of serve, do not make the mistake of retreating too great a distance into back court after completing the serve. Not only will this bad habit cause you to frequently obstruct your opponent's line of vision to the front wall, but it will make you vulnerable to corner kill shots as well as the straight kill. For the developing receiver, kill shots from back court are normally not good percentage shots, but placement is less important than usual because you as the server will have considerable difficulty retrieving kill shots from the extreme center court position.

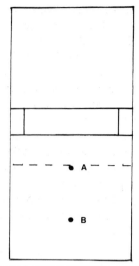

Player A obstructs player B's vision.

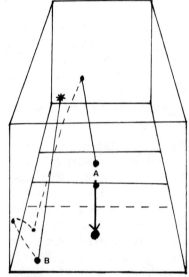

Player A retreats too far in back court after serving; player B responds with straight kill.

Setting up approximately two steps behind the short line is sufficient against a player who uses soft returns effectively or when taking advantage of an opponent who lacks good placement on service returns. About five steps into back court is an appropriate court position against a ceiling shot artist.

Mixing Service Type and Speed

Competent servers methodically vary the type and speed of serve. This way their styles of service do not become too predictable. Keeping the opponent guessing will help to maximize your proficiency in serving. In fact, it is a good idea to hit one out of every four or five serves to your opponent's forehand side to inject the surprise element into serving. That is not to say that serves to your opponent's forehand side are necessarily low percentage serves, because Z and low drive serves to that side can be effective serves when strategically used.

Soft serves are sometimes effective against players who prefer to return all types of serves with power. The opposite is true if the opponent is a practitioner of the slow-paced style of play. You should remember that hard serves are more difficult to control but have the percentage edge in effectiveness over soft serves.

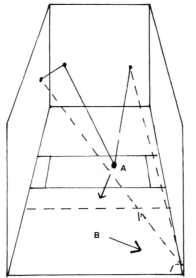

Player A employs Z serve (left) and low drive power serve (right) against player B.

All serves should be directed toward a back wall corner. This is a percentage tactic because corner balls are much more difficult to return than balls rebounding straight off the back wall. Serves bounding straight off the back wall will set up your opponent for a high percentage return. They are somewhat difficult to kill but will seldom fool your opponent like the unpredictable corner caroms tend to do.

SERVICE RETURN STRATEGY

Tips on Preparing for and Returning Service

Your major objective in learning to return serve properly is to force the server out of center court and then gain control of that relinquished area of the court. In assuming a position to await the serve, you should stand approximately two steps from the back wall about midway between the two sides of the court. Your knees should be bent to facilitate a quick reaction in any direction. Since the majority of serves are directed toward the backhand side, you may wish to shade the backhand side of the court to a reasonable degree when assuming the service return position. The latter practice is not necessarily a percentage move but rather a matter of individual preference. Some players feel that they are too vulnerable against Z and low drive serves in the right corner when favoring the backhand side of the court. Going ahead and assuming a backhand grip on the racquet is a good habit to develop, because the change from forehand to backhand grip has to be made anyway for most serves. This recommendation excludes players who prefer the Continental grip, which can be used for performing all racquetball strokes.

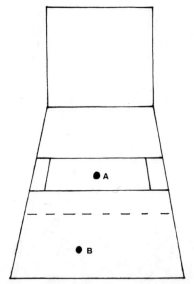

Player B shades backhand side in anticipation of player A's serve.

As the player returning serve, you must remember that all service returns should strike the front wall first, as side wall-front wall returns almost always set up the opponent for an easy shot. Furthermore, returning to the center court position immediately after returning the serve should become automatic as a part of your effort to gain court advantage on the server.

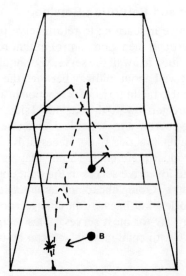

Player B's service return sets up player A.

Service Return Options

Five good shot options are available to you when returning serve: the kill, cross-court pass, down-the-wall pass, ceiling shot and around-the-wall ball. A variety of these shots should be used to avoid becoming too predictable in returning serve, especially as you become more skilled in performing the whole array.

The kill shot as a service return should be a corner kill on the side where the ball is served, but this shot is not advisable for the beginner. Even the experienced player should be very judicious in utilizing this offensive shot. It should be reserved for use when the server errs by allowing the serve to bound out into the court for an easy setup. Even then, a pass shot is a better choice if you have not yet developed an adequate kill shot. Assuming you have a good kill return and use it disproportionately with the other service return possibilities, the server will soon learn to shade the side of the court where the corner kill is overused and attempt to rekill the ball in the same corner.

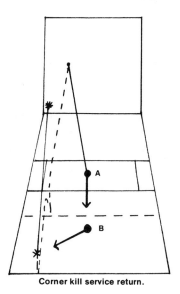

Corner kill service return.

The cross-court pass return is easier to master than the kill but is often difficult to get by the server and into the back corner. It must be a high velocity return to be successful. Otherwise, the server can cut the ball off and kill it in the corner on the same side. When the server uses a soft serve that can be comfortably volleyed before it drops into the corner area, you are presented with a good opportunity to use the cross-court pass. The same is true for serves that carom high off the back wall. These type serves are hard to kill but lend themselves well to high percentage pass shots on the opposite side. Even if you do not break serve with this shot, it will often force the server to retreat toward the back corner and thus forfeit the center court position. The cross-court pass is particularly effective against servers who are slow to leave the service box or in situations where the server overplays the side of the court where the serves are directed.

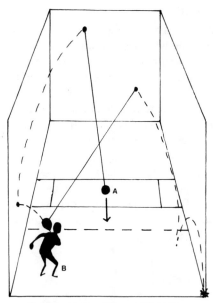

Cross-court pass return on lob serve.

The down-the-wall pass shot requires good placement to be effective but does not possess the scoring potential of the kill. However, the shot moves the server away from the middle of the court and is a rather safe return unless the server has a good backhand kill. It is also useful when the server assumes a position that favors the side of the court opposite the down-the-wall return.

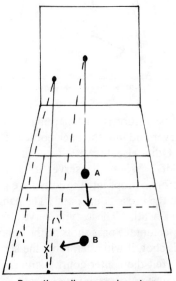

Down-the-wall pass service return.

Although its margin of placement error is small, the ceiling shot is generally your best defense against a good serve. The ceiling shot takes time for the novice player to master and should be practiced regularly, because acquisition of this valuable defensive shot is imperative if you desire to reach full playing potential. There are just too many service return situations in which the ceiling shot is the best percentage return for you not to be able to perform it adequately.

Serves rebounding off the back wall at waist level or above are good candidates for ceiling shots. Ceiling shots should not be attempted on balls dropping below the waist, as they are harder to drive up toward the ceiling. Competent players capitalize on poorly placed ceiling shots. Thus, you should avoid the tendency to overuse the ceiling shot return.

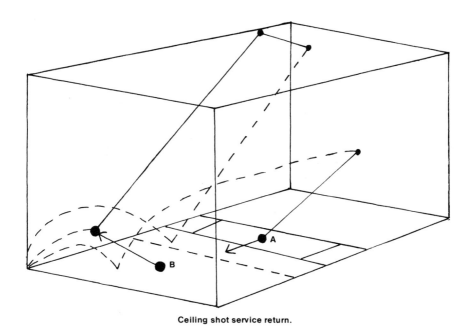

Ceiling shot service return.

An around-the-wall ball is another defensive shot in the service return repertoire of some players. The return changes the pace of the game and is recommended for use against soft serves such as the lob, garbage or high Z serve. Servers tend to make more errors in responding to this shot than to some of the other service return shots. First, they see the shot only infrequently and often become too anxious in returning the ball. Second, the ball can take unpredictable bounces if allowed to travel to the back court wall junctures.

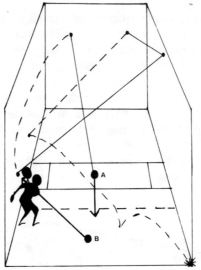

Around-the-wall ball service return on lob serve.

Proper Return of Service Setup

Learn to take full advantage of any opportunity to return serves that come off the back wall in the middle of the court. Since the server must move to one side of the court to avoid hindering your return shot, about two thirds of the court is open for a pass or pinch shot attempt. The pass shot should be hit low off the front wall so the server is unable to retreat and play the ball off the back wall. A well-placed pinch shot is virtually impossible to return from the server's precarious position.

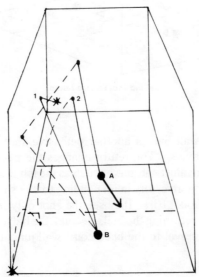

Player B has option of pinch (1) or pass (2) on player A's service setup.

Point of Contact on Service Returns

Another very important principle of the service return phase of racquetball is to hit offensive shots on balls that must be struck below the knees and use defensive shots for those contacted above the knees. It is worth repeating here that high soft serves should be hit in the air whenever possible because the chances of making a good return diminish if the ball is allowed to rebound from a back wall juncture. These soft serves frequently die in the corners, leaving you very little chance of returning them.

Choosing Between Forehand and Backhand Returns

When to select a forehand return over a backhand shot is an important fundamental that should be learned early and put into practice at every opportunity. Actually, it applies to wall play as well as during return of serve. There is universal agreement that the most difficult serves to return are those that die at the wall juncture on the opponent's backhand side before hitting the back wall. Fortunately for you when returning serve, the beginning or intermediate level server usually fails to negotiate such a serve. The serve is often hit too high into back court and is angled too much toward the side wall. As a result, the ball tends to carom off the back wall toward center court. When this happens, you have an excellent opportunity for a high percentage return. Some players err in this situation by not exploiting the opportunity to use a forehand return. Instead, they follow the ball toward the corner, then retreat and hit the ball with the backhand, a lower percentage shot.

With experience in playing, you will learn to sense where the ball will carom off the back or side wall. Balls heading straight toward the wall juncture should be hit with the backhand because they do not bound out far enough toward mid-court for you to use the forehand. Serves hitting the back wall first and rebounding off the side wall should also be returned with the backhand. Sometimes a hard serve intended for the backhand corner is angled too much toward center court and explodes off the back wall. In this instance, you must shuffle laterally for a few steps before taking a backhand return. But when the serve is angled too much toward the side wall and results in a forehand opportunity, you must be adept at completing a full pivot while following the ball around the wall juncture, resulting in a favorable forehand position. The moment you detect that the serve will take a side wall-back wall carom toward the center court area, you should initiate the pivot, follow the ball around the wall and then use whatever lateral footwork is necessary to assume a proper forehand stance for hitting the ball. Beginners should practice this maneuver earnestly in their early development so it becomes a natural reaction during competition. The knack of knowing when to choose the forehand over the backhand in returning serve pays immediate dividends and is another example of playing percentage racquetball.

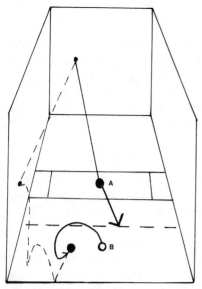

Player B assumes forehand position to return player A's poorly placed serve.

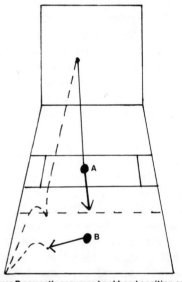

Player B correctly assumes backhand position on serve headed directly toward corner juncture.

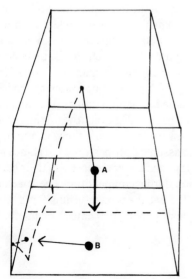

Location of carom forces player B to use backhand return.

RALLY STRATEGY

Once a serve has been returned, the ensuing exchange of shots is called a "rally." Attaining the upper hand in the center court game is the key factor toward winning the rally, but shot selection, hustle, concentration, stamina and general court sense are other important factors that help decide the winner in closely contested rallies. Patience is required for proficiency in rally competition, along with an astute blending of offensive and defensive strategy.

Ceiling Shot Rally

Rallies often develop into ceiling shot contests when a ceiling shot return of service is used. As a matter of fact, the potential for a ceiling shot contest is present any time this shot is used by one of the players. Interestingly, the most effective shot against an opponent's ceiling shot is another ceiling shot. Placement of the shot should force a backhand return, increasing the opponent's chance for error on the return. A straight kill or corner kill shot following an opponent's well-placed ceiling shot is a low percentage counter, as is the pass shot, which can be retrieved fairly easily from a back court position. Ceiling shot rallies usually end with one player performing an effective overhead kill, or when one player takes advantage of a poorly placed ceiling shot.

Response to Service Return

Pass and kill shots are effective shots for you as the server when responding to the receiver's return of service. If the receiver tries a cross-court pass shot, you must anticipate the side of the court to which the shot will be hit, step over into the passing lane, and kill the ball with a hard half-volley stroke. This shot should also be used to hit balls traveling in the air below your waist. If the receiver starts to overplay the side of the court where the kill shot is being used, then a pass shot directed toward the other side of the court is recommended. The same principles of strategy will be effective for you in defending down-the-wall pass shots.

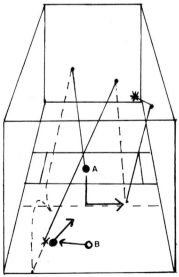

Player A cuts off player B's pass shot and counters with pinch shot.

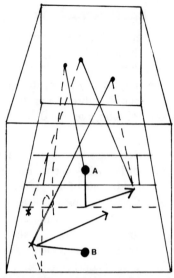

Player B returns serve with cross-court pass and sets up in right center court in anticipation of player A's corner kill; Player A responds instead with cross-court pass.

The old adage, "Fight fire with fire," describes the appropriate tactic for defending a receiver's kill shot returns. Assuming the return is not a roll-out (perfect kill) for which there is no defense, a corner kill using the half-volley motion alluded to previously is a sound counterattack against kill shot returns.

Shot Selection During Rallies

Shot selection in rally situations should be firmly based on the percentage game philosophy, with common sense dictating the type of shot offering good potential for success in each particular circumstance. Though it is tempting at times to try a low percentage shot as a surprise maneuver on the opponent, you must remember that mixing high percentage shots can also produce the surprise effect but not at the expense of good shot percentage.

Following is a list of percentage shot options available to you in various rally situations.

Your Court Position and Opponent's	*Percentage Shot Option*
You and opponent in front court	Pass
You in front court, opponent in service box	Pass, Z
You in front court, opponent in center court area	Pinch, Drop, Pass, Z
You in front court, opponent in back court	Pinch, Drop, Kill
You and opponent in service box	Pass, Z, Ceiling, Around-the-wall
You in service box, opponent in front court	Pass
You in service box, opponent in center court area	Corner kill, Ceiling, Z

You in service box, opponent in back court	Kill
You and opponent in center court area	Corner kill, Cross-court pass, Ceiling, Z, Around-the-wall
You in center court area, opponent in front court	Pass, Ceiling, Z, Around-the-wall
You in center court area, opponent in service box	Pass, Ceiling, Z, Around-the-wall
You in center court area, opponent in back court	Kill
You and opponent in back court	Ceiling, Kill
You in back court, opponent in front court	Pass, Ceiling, Around-the-wall, Z
You in back court, opponent in service box	Pass, Ceiling, Z, Around-the-wall
You in back court, opponent in center court area	Ceiling, Cross-court pass, Z, Around-the-wall

DOUBLES STRATEGY

As in singles competition, playing the percentages and controlling center court are basic to good doubles play. Doubles play is more deliberate than singles with good reason. Four players cover the court much more easily than two, which means there is less margin for error in the execution of effective offensive shots. Thus, the game promotes a conservative style of play, with the team displaying the most patience usually experiencing the most success. A doubles game ordinarily takes more time to play than singles, as ceiling ball rallies are more frequent and of greater duration.

Team Formations

Two basic formations are used for court coverage in doubles: the side-by-side and "I" formations. The side-by-side formation is the easiest to play, as this method more closely simulates singles play. You and your partner set up in a natural center court position in the side-by-side formation, while the "I" formation forces one of you to assume an unnatural position on the court. Furthermore, the side-by-side formation markedly restricts your opponents' effective use of one of the two main offensive shots in racquetball, the pass. This is a basic reason why doubles play commonly mandates a patient, deliberate style of play.

In each of the two formations, you are responsible for half of the court. When you and your partner use the side-by-side approach, one of you must cover the right side while the other is responsible for the left. A right-hander/left-hander team is ideal for this type of formation, since they can position themselves in such a way as to avoid having to use the backhand stroke on balls in the corners. The player possessing the better backhand should take shots down the middle of the court. When the dominant arm is the same for you and your partner, whoever has the superior backhand should play the side that requires use of the backhand on corner balls. Balls in the middle for this type of team should be hit by the player on the forehand side.

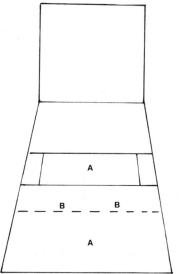

Team A in "I" formation, with team B employing side-by-side formation.

Utilization of the "I" formation is not recommended unless your team possesses the skills necessary to make that formation effective. Good front court play requires above-average reaction time and proficiency in using the half-volley stroke for executing kill and drop shots. The player assigned to cover back court must be able to properly execute shots from deep back court and be skilled at hitting the ceiling shot. Shrewd opponents inevitably identify shortcomings in the skills of the duo using the "I" formation and soon start to exploit those weaknesses. The formation is particularly vulnerable to shots in the corners and down the sides of the court, the areas where offensive shots are most effective.

Service Strategy in Doubles

Scoring on the serve is not as common in doubles as it is in singles because the receivers have less back court space to cover in completing the service return. Each player can intensely concentrate on his/her half of the court, which restricts the server's ability to deceive the opposition. However, if the serving team uses a variety of serves, some weaknesses in the opposing team may be uncovered. If one of the doubles opponents is decidedly weaker than the other, most serves should be directed to that player's weakest side. Another general principle of percentage racquetball is to direct the vast majority of serves toward the corner or corners that force opponents to use a backhand return. As mentioned earlier, sometimes one opponent is right-handed and the other left-handed, and they may set up with their forehands toward the side walls. In this instance, low drive power serves directed toward the center of the court are high percentage serves because they must be returned with a backhand stroke, and indecision often results as to which one of the opponents will attempt the return.

Service Return Strategy in Doubles

Service returns should be hit away from the stronger opponent. The safest return, especially on strong serves, is the ceiling shot. A successful ceiling return

68

will give your team the advantage in center court and force the opposition into a defensive posture.

Kill returns may be used on weak serves, and soft lob serves should be volleyed before being allowed to strike the floor. Trying a kill shot on a lob serve is not a very good percentage maneuver, since contact with the ball must usually be made above waist level. However, the ceiling shot is relatively easy to perform on lob serves and should be used frequently in that situation.

Rally Play in Doubles

A rather simple strategy evolves in the doubles game, even though the game appears somewhat complicated to the novice or casual observer of racquetball. Basically, the blanket court coverage of four players causes long ceiling ball rallies, with the victor either hitting a successful overhead kill or putting away an opponent's poorly placed ceiling shot. The doubles game boils down to a test of patience and shot placement.

Corner kill shots, especially the pinch, are the best offensive shots to use in the doubles game. Wide angle pass shots of high velocity can also be effective offensive shots, since they tend to handcuff rushing opponents or bypass those caught in front of the short line.

As recommended for the serve, the majority of shots should be directed toward the weaker opponent. This is a rule of thumb in the percentage game. In friendly racquetball, this rule of strategy can sometimes take the fun out of the game because one team may be considerably weaker in skill than the other. This is a situation where strategy becomes less important than game enjoyment. Doubles play, as is the case with all types of racquetball competition, is most enjoyable when opposing teams are close in level of ability.

CUTTHROAT STRATEGY

Any experienced performer of the three-player racquetball game knows that this type of competition is aptly named. By design, the server is forced to compete against the other two players. With three sides involved instead of two, cutthroat games tend to last longer than singles and doubles games. Players rotate service in a clockwise manner, and the first player to accumulate 21 points is the winner.

Just as in singles and doubles competition, adherence to the principles of percentage racquetball and the center court game is crucial for successful cutthroat play. Since it contains features of both singles and doubles play, the cutthroat game can be confusing to the inexperienced player, as principles of both types of play must be put into action.

Service and Service Return in Cutthroat

The principles of doubles service should be followed when serving in cutthroat play, since the receiving position of the cutthroat opponents parallels that of a doubles team. Service return strategy used in singles play is appropriate for use in cutthroat competition, but the cutthroat receivers can afford to hit the ball harder and take more risks than a singles receiver is able to do. This places a good deal of pressure on the server and helps to prevent him/her from getting in a "groove" and running off a substantial number of consecutive points.

Rally Play in Cutthroat

Through the duration of a cutthroat game, it is a good idea for you to use a conservative, deliberate style of play on offense while utilizing a contrasting style on defense when paired with another player. You must realize the difficulty of outplaying two opponents offensively and thus show patience until one of them makes a mistake that will open the door for you to make a high percentage return. Just as in doubles play, success in cutthroat competition requires the server to be proficient at using a firm half-volley return on balls arriving at waist level or below.

6

Preventing
and Rehabilitating
Racquetball Injuries

WARMING UP

Racquetball is a game that requires quickness, mobility, speed and total body movement and control. Therefore, it is important that you allow for five to ten minutes of warm-up exercises before ever entering the court. Warming up is a physiological process that allows your body temperature to increase (through controlled exercise), which in turn allows your muscles to work with greater efficiency. Warm-up prepares your body for the vigorous exercise that you will experience on the racquetball court.

Research shows that proper warm-up exercises help eliminate such common injuries as sprained ankles, sore muscles, and torn or stretched muscles, ligaments and tendons, as well as other potential bone or joint injuries.

A proper warm-up routine includes both stretching and cardiovascular exercises that involve the major muscle groups of the body. The following list of warm-up exercises is provided for your information and use. Since a detailed explanation of each is not presented here, you may need to consult your instructor for directions on performing certain exercises.

Jogging in place	Bent-knee sit-ups
Alternate toe touch	Trunk twists
Knee bends	Trunk circles
Shoulder shrugs	Rocker exercise
Seal raises	Side-straddle hops
Arm circles	Flutter kicks
Hip-thigh raises	Burpees (squat thrusts)
Hurdle stretch	Pillow jumps
Fencer's stretch	Straight-leg stretch
Push-ups	Leg lifts

Once the general warm-up is concluded, you should enter the court and begin to practice the shots required in game play. Begin by practicing the strokes slowly and softly, and gradually increase the intensity. Hitting drills directed toward actual shots should be part of the warm-up. You should spend three to five minutes engaged in hitting drills before the beginning of the match. Your instructor may teach you some basic court drills or you may refer to Chapter III, "Improving Your Skills."

Below is a list of warm-up drills:

Forehand drop and hit	Back wall forehand
Backhand drop and hit	Back wall backhand
Forehand ceiling	Forehand kill
Backhand ceiling	Backhand kill

COOLING DOWN

The importance of the cooling-down period that occurs immediately after the completion of a racquetball match is often overlooked. After a strenuous match, you should walk around for three to five minutes at a slow, easy pace. Go to the drinking fountain or take a leisurely walk to your locker. The worst thing you could do is sit or lie down on the floor immediately after leaving the court. This causes the blood to pool in the legs and slows recovery. Research studies confirm that a period of light activity (called active rest) following a strenuous bout of exercise hastens the body's return to a normal resting state.

CAUSE AND PREVENTION OF SELECTED INJURIES

Many avoidable racquetball injuries involve the eyes. The relatively high incidence of eye injuries in racquetball clearly illustrates the importance of using protective eyewear.

The high-speed forehand and backhand strokes greatly increase the chances of muscle injuries. While some injuries occur to the rear leg, stride leg and non-racquet arm, this section focuses on common racquet arm injuries. These injuries fall into the six general categories of anterior shoulder, inside elbow, posterior elbow, posterior shoulder, outside elbow and wrist.

Anterior shoulder. In the forehand power strokes, some players point the racquet forward and downward through the fully prepared position. Therefore, when the racquet arm drives forward, it twists to point the racquet generally upward and backward. This twisting strains the muscles of the anterior shoulder by "elastic rebound." Elastic rebound describes the muscle action of the anterior shoulder when the weight of the racquet forces the arm backward while the arm drives forward. To prevent elastic rebound, a player should ease the racquet arm through the fully prepared position very early, with the racquet pointing generally upward and backward.

Allowing the body to drift forward over the stride foot also strains the muscles of the anterior shoulder. To prevent this strain, a player should rotate about a single vertical axis by pushing vigorously against the stride foot.

Inside elbow. "Little League elbow" involves injury to the muscles of the inside elbow area. The inside elbow muscles prevent the forearm from ripping away from the upper arm during the fully cocked moment of the forehand power strokes. Elimination of elastic rebound reduces this injury potential.

Racquet arm fully cocked for the forehand power stroke. Anterior shoulder and inside elbow injury potential.

Posterior elbow. The weight of the racquet during the forehand power stroke straightens the elbow immediately after ball contact. To avoid this injury, a player should raise the elbow immediately after ball contact. Furthermore, the player should keep the elbow slightly bent throughout these strokes.

Immediately after ball contact. Posterior elbow injury potential.

The weight of the racquet during the backhand power strokes straightens the elbow immediately after ball contact. To avoid this injury, a player should lower the elbow as soon as possible after ball contact. The player should also keep the elbow slightly bent throughout these strokes.

Racquet contact with ball. Posterior elbow injury potential.

Posterior shoulder. The structure of the human shoulder allows the upper arm to rotate forward more easily than backward. Therefore, elastic rebound during the backhand does not strain the posterior shoulder as severely as elastic rebound during the forehand power strokes. During the backhand power strokes elastic rebound also causes a looping of the racquet below the level of ball contact. To avoid this looping, a player should ease the racquet arm through the fully prepared position with the racquet pointing generally backward and upward.

Racquet arm fully cocked for backhand power stroke. Posterior shoulder, outside elbow and wrist injury potential.

Outside elbow. "Tennis elbow" involves injury to the muscles of the outside elbow area. The outside elbow muscles prevent the forearm from ripping away from the upper arm during the fully cocked moment of the backhand power strokes. Elimination of elastic rebound reduces this injury potential.

Wrist. Elastic rebound creates a loop in the beginning phase of the backhand power strokes. This looping strains the attachments of the muscles of the thumb that drive the racquet to ball contact. Again, elimination of elastic rebound reduces this injury potential.

Racquet arm fully cocked for backhand power stroke. Posterior shoulder, outside elbow and wrist injury potential.

REHABILITATION

Muscle soreness results from minor muscle fiber tears that usually heal in a day or two without therapy. However, when muscle fibers tear more severely, adjoining muscle fibers form a protective shield by sustaining a continuous contraction. This shield prevents needed blood flow to the injured muscle fibers within. When the injury is palpated, this protective shield feels like a strand of rope. Sometimes a portion of a tendon pulls slightly from its attachment to the bone. These injuries require several months of therapy before the pain subsides completely. Since only broken bones and surgically reattached ligaments and tendons require immobilization, players should increase blood flow to the injury for all degrees of muscle tears.

In their order of effectiveness, 1) measured exercise overload, 2) cold-induced vasodilation (CIVD) and 3) deep muscle massage increase blood flow to a specific portion of the body.

In measured exercise overload, trained professionals design an exercise program to measuredly stress the injury. Muscle contraction creates an oxygen debt that in turn relaxes the muscle fibers of the protective shield. Then, the blood flow increases to the injury. Reactive hyperemia is the physiological name for this phenomenon.

Cold-induced vasodilation means placing an ice pack on the injury. While the initial response is vasoconstriction (blood vessels closing down), after a few minutes the muscle fibers require the oxygen that they are not receiving. At this point, reactive hyperemia again increases blood flow to the injury by dilating (opening) the blood vessels.

In deep muscle massage, rubbing the injury firmly applies pressure to the contracted muscle fibers of the protective shield. While care should be taken not to bruise the muscle, firm, deep muscle massage relaxes the contracted muscle fibers and thereby increases blood flow to the injury.

After these therapies help the natural rehabilitation processes and the injured area feels strong enough to practice the strokes gently, a player should perform the various racquetball strokes with minimum intensity for 50 to 100 repetitions daily. Then, while taking care not to rush the recovery, the player should gradually increase the intensity of workouts on subsequent days.

7

Evaluating Your Progress

SKILLS TESTING

The five skills test items in this chapter are designed to measure a player's overall racquetball ability when administered in total. A wall volley test item and skill items for the serve, kill, ceiling and back wall placement are included.

The wall volley test item measures an individual's ability to control the racquet when stroking the ball, a skill that is common to general racquetball ability. More specifically, the wall volley test measures accuracy in shot placement and, to a lesser degree, the speed component of racquetball. Racquetball instructors will find the wall volley test useful for teaching purposes, to classify students by ability level early in a course.

Measurement of student achievement is one obvious application of all the test items. Each of the five test items may be used by instructors as excellent motivators for student improvement, as the monitoring of individual progress through self-testing is often the single greatest contributor to success in sports skills achievement. These test items can also be valuable teaching aids for the instructor, because they provide a ready check of student progress in skills development and may reveal areas needing increased instructional emphasis.

The serve, ceiling, kill and back wall placement items are valuable as practice drills for students learning how to successfully perform those shots. Therefore, it is a good idea for instructors to maintain permanent court markings in at least one court.

The wall volley and serve items can be effectively used in testing players of any ability level, while the ceiling, kill and back wall placement items are particularly useful in testing intermediate and advanced level performers.

The value of the wall volley test item as an indicator of overall racquetball ability was substantiated in a study involving 51 college men. Each student was assigned an ability rating by four experienced racquetball instructors, which was correlated with the student's test score. An acceptable statistical relationship was determined. Reliability of this item was confirmed, as the scores of the 51 students on separate tests were highly consistent.

The serve item demonstrates face validity, as the placement skill required is the same as that involved in actual game play. Speed of the serve is not measured, but this is not considered a significant shortcoming because a well-placed serve can be effective at any speed. Furthermore, placement should receive more attention than speed in teaching the serve to beginners.

A defensible claim of face validity can also be made for the ceiling, kill and back wall placement test items, since the skill requirements so closely simulate those needed in a game situation.

Administrative Feasibility of Test Items

Utilizing one court, the wall volley test can be administered to 15 students in 45 minutes. Each of the other items requires a similar amount of time, provided the testing is limited to one court. Should the instructor choose to administer more than one item, a rotational system can be effectively implemented through the employment of trained assistants. With the availability of five courts or more, at least 15 students could be tested on all five items in a 45-minute class period.

Ideally, the instructor should serve as scorer-recorder for each test item. During the wall volley test, he/she should be in a position to immediately hand the student a second ball should the original one get away. A trained student assistant can effectively serve as timer for the wall volley test. In a mass-testing situation involving the use of multiple courts, trained student assistants may be used as scorer-recorders.

Necessary equipment for test administration includes an ample supply of racquets, at least three good-quality racquetballs and one stopwatch per court used. A wristwatch with a sweep secondhand suffices in the absence of a stopwatch. Materials for recording the test scores are necessary accessories.

A sufficient amount of uniform practice time should be allowed for each student in class periods that precede a day of testing. A brief uniform practice period should also be allotted for each student on the test date.

Directions for Administering Test Items

WALL VOLLEY

The subject assumes a position behind the short line, drops the ball to the floor and rallies continuously for 30 seconds. The ball must be hit after one bounce, with a violation occurring either when the ball bounces two or more times, when the ball is hit in the air, or when the subject steps on or over the short line. If the ball gets away from the subject, the instructor provides another immediately by directly handing a ball to the subject. The subject resumes the test in the same manner as at the beginning. The test does not have to be restarted on a violation, only if the ball gets away from the subject. Although a disadvantage to the subject, the ball may hit the side wall or ceiling as long as the front wall is struck. Any type of stroke may be used. The stopwatch should start the instant the ball touches the floor when dropped by the subject to initiate the test. Only the number of hits within the 30-second time period count for score.

The final score is the number of successful hits made in 30 seconds. The instructor should serve as scorer-recorder, with a student assistant used as timer.

There are alternatives to having someone hand another ball to the subject if the original test ball gets away. A tester may design the test so that the subject holds a second ball in the non-racquet hand until it is needed. Or the tester may opt for a ball container to be placed on each side of the racquetball court, directly behind the short line of the service zone. In any event, a trial should be repeated if the tester feels that an undue amount of time is allowed to expire while a second ball is being put into play, placing the student in an unfair position when his/her score is compared to peer scores.

Whatever method is used for putting the second ball into play, the tester is reminded that its application should be consistent for the entire test group, and the development and use of norms from individual test scores should be specific to the particular method used.

SERVE

Standing in the service area, the subject attempts ten serves, five to each side of the court. Considering that placement is the primary objective in serving, any type of serve may be used. An illegal serve counts as a trial and is given a zero score. Points are assigned according to the scoring area (floor) where the ball hits after the initial bounce. Balls hitting a line are given the higher point value. The line running through scoring areas three (3 points) and one (1 point) serves as the boundary for the right and left sides. Balls must be served to the designated side to score.

Fifty points is the maximum score. The instructor should serve as scorer-recorder.

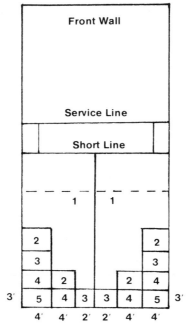

Court markings for serve and ceiling test items.

CEILING

The subject assumes a position in the back court, while the instructor stands directly behind the short line on the side opposite the racquet hand of the subject. The instructor tosses the ball against the front wall so that after the first bounce it can be comfortably struck by the subject standing in the back court. Ten trials are completed with the racquet hand. The ball may hit the front wall first as long as the ceiling is struck. If the ball does not hit the ceiling, a trial is counted and is

81

given a zero score. Points are assigned according to the scoring area (floor) where the ball hits after the initial bounce. A ball hitting a line is assigned the higher point value. A retrial occurs when the instructor judges a toss to be poorly thrown or when the subject hits the ball while standing on or in front of the short line.

The maximum score is 50 points. The instructor serves as scorer, with a student assistant recording the scores.

KILL

The subject assumes a position in the back court, while the instructor stands directly behind the short line on the side opposite the subject's hitting side. The instructor tosses the ball against the front wall so that after the first bounce it can be comfortably struck by the subject standing in the back court. Ten trials are completed, five with the forehand and the same number with the backhand. A retrial occurs when the instructor judges a toss to be poorly thrown or when the subject hits the ball while standing on or in front of the short line. Balls may hit the side walls first, but those initially hitting the ceiling or floor count as zero. Each trial is scored according to the ball's point of contact on the front wall scoring area, with the higher value allowed for balls striking a line.

The maximum score is 50 points. The instructor serves as scorer, with a student assistant recording the scores.

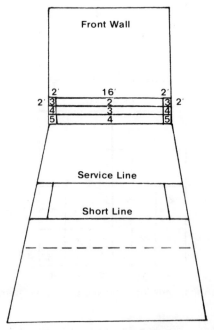

Court markings for kill and back wall placement test items.

BACK WALL PLACEMENT

The subject assumes a position in the back court, while the instructor stands directly behind the short line on the same side as the subject's hitting side. The instructor bounces the ball on the floor so that it rebounds off the back wall in a manner that allows the subject to comfortably strike the ball. Ten trials are completed, five with the forehand and the same number with the backhand. A retrial occurs when the instructor judges a toss to be poorly thrown or when the subject hits the ball while standing on or in front of the short line. Balls may hit the side wall first, but those initially hitting the ceiling or floor count as zero. Each trial is assigned a point value based on the ball's point of contact on the front wall scoring area. Balls striking a line are given the score of higher value.

The maximum score is 50 points. The instructor serves as scorer, with a student assistant recording the scores.

Achievement Scale for Racquetball Wall Volley Test

The following achievement scale is presented as a reference for potential users of the wall volley test. The men's performance on two trials of the test produced a mean of 28.3, while the mean for the women was 21.4.

Performance Level	Men	Women
Excellent	45 & above	37 & above
Above Average	37-44	29-36
Average	21-36	15-28
Below Average	13-20	7-14
Poor	12 & below	6 & below

(Based on scores of 198 college men and 222 college women.)

SAMPLE SCORE SHEET FOR SKILLS TEST

Instructor _____ Course title and # _____

Day & Time _____ Semester/Quarter _____

Name	Test 1 Wall Volley	Test 2 Serve	Test 3 Ceiling	Test 4 Kill	Test 5 Back Wall Placement	Total
1. _____ _____		RT		FH	FH	_____
		LT		BH	BH	
2. _____ _____		RT		FH	FH	_____
		LT		BH	BH	
3. _____ _____		RT		FH	FH	_____
		LT		BH	BH	
4. _____ _____		RT		FH	FH	_____
		LT		BH	BH	

83

CHECKING YOUR KNOWLEDGE

A thorough understanding of rules, etiquette and strategy of racquetball should be one of the goals for any developing player. Insight into these facets of the game will greatly complement the skill component of your game.

The following knowledge test is a teaching aid designed to help you increase your understanding of racquetball. Questions on the test were derived from the information presented in this text. Completing the test before and after reading the book and then comparing scores is an interesting exercise you may wish to do. By the end of your racquetball course, you should settle for nothing less than a 100 percent score on the test.

KNOWLEDGE TEST

True-False Place T or F in blank at left. Answer is on page indicated.

T___ 1. The form of racquetball played today has an American origin (p. 1).

T___ 2. The concept of racquetball was derived from certain elements of the older sport of tennis (p. 2).

T___ 3. Racquetball used to be known as "paddle-rackets" (p. 2).

T___ 4. The sport of racquetball has gone by that name since the late 1960s (p. 2).

T___ 5. A longer racquet allows for greater racquet control (p. 4).

T___ 6. There is a trend today toward the use of lighter racquets (p. 4).

F___ 7. Leather racquet grips last longer than those made of rubber (p. 4).

T___ 8. Leather grips provide a more secure handhold than rubber grips (p. 4).

T___ 9. Most racquets are strung between 30 and 40 pounds (p. 4).

F___ 10. Gut is the most common type of racquet string (p. 4).

F___ 11. Racquetball gloves are required during play at most racquetball clubs (p. 5).

F___ 12. The official rules of racquetball permit an overtime session when needed (p. 7).

F___ 13. The server is responsible for calling out his/her score only (p. 9).

F___ 14. It is poor etiquette for doubles partners to talk to each other during a game (p. 9).

T___ 15. Continuing to walk for a few minutes after play hastens the body's recovery from a strenuous match (p. 72).

T___ 16. Racquetball players may grip the racquet as many as four different ways for hitting the various shots (p. 10).

T___ 17. Some players prefer only one type of grip for all strokes (p. 10).

F___ 18. Some players prefer the Western grip for hitting the forehand kill shot (p. 11).

F___ 19. The most potent offensive weapon in racquetball is the pass shot (p. 13).

F___ 20. Only two types of kill shots are used in racquetball (p. 13).

F___ 21. The half-volley should be used only as a last resort (p. 13).

T___ 22. The backswing of the half-volley is shorter than that of a regular forehand stroke (p. 13).

T___ 23. Racquetball's most common defensive stroke is the ceiling shot (p. 14).

T___ 24. The best defense against a ceiling shot is another ceiling ball (p. 14).

F___ 25. A Z ball is an effective offensive shot (p. 14).

T___ 26. An example of a low percentage shot is the lob (p. 15).

T___ 27. The back-to-back wall shot should be used only as a last resort (p. 15).

FT___ 28. When performing the low drive power serve, or any racquetball stroke for that matter, the stride leg should move forward in a straight line (p. 16).

F___ 29. When the stride leg hits the floor, it should be in a straightened position (p. 17).

T___ 30. In performing a power serve, the upper arm snap of the racquet arm whips the forearm and racquet to ball contact (p. 16).

T___ 31. Strain on the elbow during the power serve stroke may be reduced by lifting the racquet elbow upward immediately after ball contact (p. 16).

84

_____ 32. During the lob serve the body is relatively upright compared to the low drive power serve (p. 21).

_____ 33. Racquet arm action during the performance of the low drive power serve parallels the action of an underarmed baseball pitch (p. 16).

_____ 34. The top of the backswing should be accentuated during the lob serve (p. 21).

_____ 35. In the lob serve, a high racquet velocity is not needed (p. 21).

_____ 36. The forehand ceiling shot should be struck with maximum power (p. 25).

_____ 37. Turning the head and upper body to almost face the back wall facilitates effective execution of a back wall return (p. 23).

_____ 38. Allowing the body to drift forward during the twisting torso phase of a stroke improves the stroke's mechanics (p. 73).

_____ 39. On a back wall return, ball contact should be made between the knee and waist (p. 46).

_____ 40. The rear arm of the backhand acts as a counterbalance to the racquet arm (p. 26).

_____ 41. The "center court" area is actually located in back court (p. 44).

_____ 42. Watching the opponent set up for a shot is an important factor in attaining good court position (p. 45).

_____ 43. The typical racquetball player can move backward on the court much faster than forward (p. 45).

_____ 44. Underhanded shots demonstrate higher percentage for scoring and breaking serve than overhanded shots (p. 46).

_____ 45. Generally, a racquetball caroms off a wall at the same angle it strikes the wall (p. 46).

_____ 46. A kill shot is a poor shot selection when the opponent is in front court (p. 49).

_____ 47. Diagonal kill shots are more effective than straight kills (p. 50).

_____ 48. Oftentimes, there simply is no effective defense for a well-placed offensive shot (p. 53).

_____ 49. Proponents of "percentage" racquetball serve near the center area of the service zone (p. 54).

_____ 50. Serving to the opponent's forehand side is poor strategy (p. 56).

_____ 51. Serves bounding straight off the back wall set up the opponent for a high percentage return (p. 57).

_____ 52. Shading the backhand side on the service return is poor strategy (p. 57).

_____ 53. Side wall-front wall service returns are effective (p. 58).

_____ 54. The cross-court pass service return must be a high velocity shot to be successful (p. 59).

_____ 55. The ceiling shot is generally the best defense against a good serve (p. 61).

_____ 56. Rallies often develop into ceiling shot contests (p. 65).

_____ 57. A half-volley corner kill is a sound counterattack against kill shot service returns (p. 66).

_____ 58. When you and your opponent are in front court, the pass is your best percentage shot option (p. 66).

_____ 59. When you are in front court and your opponent is in the service zone area, a percentage shot option available to you is the ceiling shot (p. 66).

_____ 60. When you are in the center court area and your opponent is in back court, a kill shot is your best choice (p. 67).

_____ 61. When you are in back court and your opponent is in the center court area, a defensive shot is your percentage shot option (p. 67).

_____ 62. A doubles game ordinarily takes more time to play than singles (p. 67).

_____ 63. Two basic types of team formations are used in doubles (p. 67).

_____ 64. Scoring on the serve is not as common in doubles as in singles (p. 68).

_____ 65. Down-the-wall pass shots are the best offensive shots to use in the doubles game (p. 69).

_____ 66. The three-person game is called "cutthroat" (p. 69).

_____ 67. Eye injuries are rare in racquetball (p. 72).

_____ 68. Warm-up prior to a racquetball match has no physiological benefits (p. 71).

_F_ 69. The immediate placement of a cold pack on a muscle injury tends to further damage the injured area (p. 78).

_T_ 70. Overextending the racquet upper arm and shoulder on the backswing is known as "looping" (p. 75).

_F_ 71. A player should keep the elbow slightly bent throughout the forehand and backhand strokes to avoid injury (p. 74).

_T_ 72. Rest alone will heal minor muscle injuries sustained in racquetball (p. 77).

_F_ 73. The cutthroat game is not recognized in official racquetball rules (p. 109).

_T_ 74. Points are scored only by the serving side (p. 109).

_T_ 75. Stepping on the short line while serving is permitted (p. 112).

_F_ 76. A screen ball is a fault (p. 113).

_F_ 77. A short serve is an out serve (p. 113).

_T_ 78. A crotch serve (front wall) is an out (p. 113).

_T_ 79. A crotch serve (back wall) is good and in play (p. 113).

_T_ 80. Switching hands to hit a ball is an out (p. 114).

_F_ 81. Partners on a doubles team must alternate returns during a game (p. 115).

_T_ 82. Screen balls should be replayed (p. 115).

_T_ 83. A court hinder is one type of dead ball hinder (p. 115).

_F_ 84. It is not a hinder when one player interferes with a teammate (p. 115).

_T_ 85. An avoidable hinder results in an out or point (p. 116).

_T_ 86. A game played under official rules is won by the side first scoring 15 points (p. 109).

_T_ 87. The length of a regulation four-wall racquetball court is double the width (p. 109).

_T_ 88. A regulation racquet must include a thong (p. 110).

_F_ 89. Protective eyewear is required of only certain age groups in American Amateur Racquetball Association sanctioned events (p. 110).

_F_ 90. A serve may strike the side wall first as long as it hits the front wall (p. 112).

_T_ 91. A ball going behind the server's partner in doubles is an automatic screen serve and is replayed (p. 113).

_T_ 92. A dead ball serve results in no penalty (p. 113).

_F_ 93. One fault serve results in a hand-out (p. 113).

_F_ 94. A screen ball on the serve is not a type of dead ball serve (p. 113).

_F_ 95. A long serve carries a more severe penalty than a short serve does (p. 113).

_T_ 96. A ceiling serve is a fault serve as is the three-wall serve (p. 113).

_T_ 97. A receiver must stand at least five feet back of the short line (p. 114).

_T_ 98. A receiver may return a serve before the ball hits the floor or a wall (p. 114).

_F_ 99. A back-to-back wall service return is illegal (p. 114).

_T_ 100. Both hands may be placed on the racquet when hitting the ball (p. 114).

Multiple-Choice Circle proper letter. Answer is on page indicated.

1. One of these men has been labeled the "Father of Racquetball" (p. 2).
   a. Earl Riskey
   b. Joe Sobeck
   c. Robert Kendler
   d. Charles Brumfield

2. Year racquetball was officially named (p. 2).
   a. 1929
   b. 1949
   c. 1959
   d. 1969

3. Name racquetball was known by for about two decades (p. 2).
   a. paddleball
   b. handball
   c. paddle-rackets
   d. tennis

4. One is *not* a type of racquet head design (p. 3).

   a. oval
   b. quadriform
   c. square
   d. teardrop

5. Which method is *not* used to determine serve in non-tournament play (p. 9)?

   a. lagging
   b. coin toss
   c. agreement of players
   d. player arriving first

6. Grip designed *only* for hitting ceiling shot (p. 11).

   a. Eastern
   b. Western
   c. Continental
   d. Northern

7. One of these serves is particularly effective on the receiver's forehand side (p. 12).

   a. Z
   b. half-lob
   c. lob
   d. garbage

8. Which stroke is an offensive shot (p. 13)?

   a. around-the-wall ball
   b. lob
   c. Z ball
   d. pinch

9. Injury to the outside elbow is called (p. 76) —

   a. elastic rebound
   b. tennis elbow
   c. Little League elbow
   d. looping

10. Injury to the inside elbow is called (p. 73) —

    a. elastic rebound
    b. tennis elbow
    c. Little League elbow
    d. looping

11. One is *not* a racquetball fundamental (pp. 45 & 49).

    a. Cut off all balls that can be reached.
    b. Set up for shot with knees bent.
    c. Anticipate opponent's next move.
    d. Watch opponent set up for shot.

12. Which shot has the least chance of success (p. 50)?

    a. pass from front court
    b. around-the-wall ball
    c. pinch from deep back court
    d. comer kill

13. Poorest shot selection when opponent is in front court (p. 49).

    a. around-the-wall ball
    b. ceiling
    c. pass
    d. kill

14. The down-the-wall pass shot (p. 60) —

    a.   is a rather safe return.

    b.   requires good placement to be effective.

    c.   moves the server away from the middle of the court.

    (d.) does all of the above.

15. One action violates a principle of service return strategy (p. 61 & 63).

    (a.) Use around-the-wall ball return as often as possible.

    b.   Hit offensive shots on balls below the knees.

    c.   Hit defensive shots on balls above the knees.

    d.   High lob serves should be hit on the fly whenever possible.

16. Most effective for ending a ceiling shot rally (p. 65).

    a.   pinch

    (b.) overhead kill

    c.   around-the-wall ball

    d.   cross-court pass

17. One is *not* a recommended rehabilitative method for increasing blood flow into an injured muscle (p. 77).

    a.   measured exercise overload

    b.   cold-induced vasodilation

    (c.) sauna exposure

    d.   deep muscle massage

18. Who has the option of serving in the third game (p. 112)?

    a.   player serving first in initial game

    b.   player serving second in initial game

    c.   winner of special coin toss

    (d.) player with most combined points in games one and two

19. Which of the following is an out serve (p. 113)?

    a.   short serve

    b.   long serve

    (c.) front wall crotch serve

    d.   serve touching ceiling after hitting front wall

20. Which of the following is *not* a dead ball hinder (p. 115)?

    (a.) court hinder

    b.   avoidable hinder

    c.   screen ball

    d.   backswing hinder

21. When a serve hits the server, it is (p. 113) —

    a.   dead

    b.   served again

    (c.) a side-out

    d.   ruled a hinder

22. The defensive ceiling shot can be quickly converted into which offensive shot (p. 51)?

    a.   pass shot

    b.   pinch shot

    c.   roll-out

    (d.) overhead kill

23. Stepping out of the service zone while serving constitutes a (p. 113) —

    a.   point for receiver

    b.   side-out

    (c.) fault

    d.   hinder

24. One of these statements is false (p. 68).
    a. A server may stand anywhere in the service zone while serving.
    (b.) The server must alternate serves from side to side in doubles play.
    c. A serve which appears to be long may be played at the discretion of the receiver.
    d. A partner's interference is not a hinder.

25. One of these statements is true (p. 49).
    a. A player may hit the ball more than once, provided that the ball does not touch the floor before hitting the front wall.
    b. Good singles strategy allows for an equal division of serves to the receiver's forehand and backhand.
    c. In doubles, each team member receives one serve throughout the match.
    (d.) While in center court position, a rule of thumb is to volley those balls arriving on the fly below waist level.

Matching Place proper letter in blank at left. Answer is on page indicated.

_D_ 1. ace (p. 90)	a.	best percentage defensive shot
_A_ 2. ceiling shot (p. 14)	b.	a type of two-wall kill
_C_ 3. half-lob serve (p. 12)	c.	garbage serve
_E_ 4. kill (p. 13)	d.	serve bouncing twice before receiver can return it
_B_ 5. pinch (p. 94)	e.	one of two common offensive shots
_J_ 6. plum (p. 94)	f.	three-wall defensive shot
_I_ 7. roll-out (p. 94)	g.	shot bouncing twice before opponent retrieves it
_G_ 8. winner (p. 96)	h.	two-wall diagonal serve
_F_ 9. Z ball (p. 96)	i.	perfect kill shot
_H_ 10. Z serve (p. 96)	j.	easy setup
	k.	same as V shot
	l.	same as a skip ball

Glossary
of Racquetball Terms

AARA: American Amateur Racquetball Association, the governing body of amateur racquetball (formerly International Racquetball Association).

"A" player: Player whose skill level is very advanced. Sometimes used synonymously with the term "open player." Varies locally.

Ace: Legal serve that eludes the receiver. One point is scored.

Advantage position: Center court position; position from which kill and pass shots are best executed.

Apex: Highest point in a bounce.

Appeal: The call for further judgment when one player disagrees with the referee's call.

Around-the-wall return: An around-the-wall ball used as a service return.

Around-the-wall shot: A defensive shot that hits a side wall, the front wall, and the other side wall, in that order, before touching the floor.

Avoidable hinder: An interference with the opponent's play that could have been prevented or avoided; can be intentional or unintentional.

"B" player: Player whose skill level is average or intermediate. Varies locally.

Back court: Court area between the short line and the back wall.

Backhand: Fundamental stroke hit across the body, starting on the side opposite the racquet hand. A right-hander's backhand stroke is from left to right across his/her body.

Backhand corner: Area of the court where a side wall and the back wall meet; the same side as the player's backhand.

Backhand grip: The way the hand grasps the racquet for the backhand stroke.

Backspin: Ball rotation that has reverse or bottom spin.

Backswing: Preparatory part of a stroke in which the racquet is taken back to the ready position.

Back wall: The rear wall of a court.

Back wall shot: A shot made on a ball rebounding off the rear wall.

Block: A court maneuver that prevents an opponent from viewing the ball. Also called a screen.

Bumper guard: Protective covering attached to the rim of the racquet head.

Butt: The enlarged bottom end of the racquet handle.

"C" player: Player whose skill level is at the basic or fundamental level; the advanced beginner level. Varies locally.

Ceiling ball: A ball that hits the ceiling first, then the front wall (or reverse), rebounding to deep court.

Ceiling return: A ceiling ball used as a service return.

Ceiling serve: A serve that hits the ceiling after hitting the front wall.

Center court: The area of the court just behind the short line, midway between the side walls.

Center court control: Maintaining position in center court area and forcing an opponent to retrieve balls in deep court.

Center court position: Same as advantage position.

Change-of-pace shot: Any shot hit softer than normal.

Choke: (1) To move the hand up or down on the racquet handle; (2) To "psych out" during a match.

Closed face: A racquet face angle whereby the strong surface slants toward the floor.

Cock position: The ready position of the wrist in preparation for hitting the ball.

Contact zone: The area in which the ball is normally hit with the racquet.

Control: Ability to hit the ball to an intended spot.

Control player: A player who relies primarily on shot placement rather than on the force (power) of shots.

Corner shot: Any shot that hits at or near one of the two front corners.

Court hinder: An unavoidable hinder brought about by an obstacle in the court. Point is replayed.

Crack shot: A ball that hits in the crack juncture between the floor and the side or rear wall.

Cross-court drive return: A relatively hard-hit service return that hits the front wall and passes the server on the opposite side from which the shot came.

Cross-court pass shot: Pass shot hit from the left side of the court to the right, or from the right to the left.

Crotch: The line juncture at which two flat surfaces of the court join. An example is the floor-side wall crotch.

Crotch serve: An illegal serve that strikes the juncture of the front wall and the floor or ceiling.

Crotch shot: A shot that hits the juncture of any two playing surfaces.

Crowding: Playing too close to an opponent.

Cutthroat: A game involving three players in which the server plays against the other two players.

Dead ball: A ball that is no longer in play.

Defensive shot: A return shot designed to continue a rally rather than end it.

Dig: To retrieve a low shot before it strikes the floor twice.

Donut: To hold the opponent to zero points.

Doubles: A form of racquetball in which two teams composed of two players each compete.

Downswing: The forward and downward motion of the racquet from the top of the backswing to the point of contact.

Down-the-wall shot: A shot hit near a side wall, which hits the front wall directly, then rebounds back along the same side wall.

Drive: A powerfully hit ball that travels in a straight line.

Drive serve: A relatively hard-hit serve that strikes the front wall and rebounds in a straight line to deep court.

Drop shot: A shot that is hit with very little force and rebounds only a few feet from the front wall.

English: Another term for the spin imparted to a ball by the racquet.

Error: Failure to return an apparently playable ball.

Exchange: The change in positions of two singles players following the end of a rally. The server becomes the receiver and vice versa.

Face: The hitting surface of the racquet; the plane formed by the racquet strings.

Fault: An illegal serve or infraction of the rules while serving. Two faults result in a side-out.

Five-foot line: The broken line five feet behind and parallel to the short line. Also called receiving line.

Float: A ball that travels so slowly that the opponent has enough time to set up for his next shot.

Fly ball: Any shot taken before a floor bounce; hit directly on the rebound off the front or side wall; also called a volley shot.

Follow-through: The continuation of the swing after contact is made with the ball.

Foot fault: An illegal position whereby the server's foot is outside the service zone during the serve.

Footwork: Movement of the feet during play; usually denotes foot movement while setting up to hit a shot.

Forehand: Fundamental stroke hit across the body from the same side as the racquet hand. A right-hander's forehand stroke is from right to left across his/her body.

Forehand grip: The manner by which a player grasps the racquet to hit forehand shots.

Four-wall racquetball: The most popular variety of the game, as opposed to three-wall or one-wall racquetball. In four-wall racquetball, the ball is played off the four walls, the ceiling and the floor.

Front court: The first 15 feet of the court, from the front wall to the service line.

Front wall-side wall kill: A kill shot that hits and rebounds off the front wall, touches either side wall and rebounds in such a way that the opponent is unable to retrieve the ball.

Game: The portion of a match that is completed when one player or team reaches 15 points.

Gamesmanship: The use of unusual, dubious or psychological tactics on or off the court to gain a winning edge.

Garbage serve: A half-speed serve that hits midway up on the front wall and returns to the receiver at near shoulder height in either of the rear court corners.

Grip: The manner in which the racquet handle is grasped; the cover material of the racquet handle that prevents slippage.

Half-lob serve: Same as garbage serve.

Half-volley: A firm, compact stroke utilizing a short backswing and follow-through. Also, to hit the ball on a short hop or just after it bounces on the floor.

Hand-out: Loss of serve by partner serving first for doubles team.

Handshake grip: The most common method of gripping the racquet, likened to shaking hands with a person.

Head: The hitting surface of the racquet, including the rim and strung face.

Hinder: An unintentional interference or screen of a ball so that the opponent does not have a fair chance to make a return. The point is replayed without penalty.

"I" formation: One method of dividing court responsibilities between the two players of a doubles team. An imaginary line is drawn from side wall to side wall; one player covers the front court and the other the back court. Also called the front-and-back formation.

Inning: A round of play in singles in which both players have served, or in doubles when both players of each team have served.

IRA: International Racquetball Association; no longer exists.

Isolation strategy: The hitting of several consecutive shots to one player in doubles and very few to his/her partner.

Kill shot: An offensive shot that hits the front wall so low that a return by the opponent is impossible.

Line judge: One of two referees' aides who are called upon to judge an appeal call made by one of the players.

Live ball: A ball still in play, as opposed to a dead ball; a racquetball that is fast or has a high bounce.

Lob shot: A shot hit high and gently toward the front wall, which rebounds to the back wall in a high arc (often used as a serve).

Long serve: A serve that rebounds to the back wall without hitting the floor. This is a fault.

Match: A complete racquetball contest, composed of the best two out of three games.

Mid-court: The area of the court between the service line and the receiving line.

Non-front serve: A serve that hits any surface other than the front wall before hitting the front wall. This serve is illegal, and the penalty is loss of service.

Novice: A relatively low skilled player or a true beginner at the sport; sometimes synonymous with "C" player.

NRC: National Racquetball Club; no longer exists.

Offensive position: Center court position, the most desirable spot for offensive play. Same as advantage or percentage position.

Offensive shot: Any shot intended either to end the rally immediately or to put the opponent in a weak court position; usually a kill or pass shot.

Off hand: Non-racquet hand.

One-on-two: Game with three players in which the server plays the other two for the entirety of the game.

One-wall racquetball: An outdoor variety of the sport in which only a front wall is utilized.

Open face: The angle of the racquet upon ball contact whereby the hitting surface is slanted toward the ceiling; this causes unwanted slicing or backspin on the ball.

Overhead: A shot hit at shoulder level or higher.

Paddleball: Racquetball's immediate predecessor, which is played on the same court and with the same rules as racquetball, but a wooden paddle and different ball are used.

Pass shot: A shot hit past an opponent out of his/her reach; may be cross-court or down-the-wall type. Also called a drive shot.

Pinch shot: A kill shot that hits a side wall, then the front wall.

Plum: A ball that can be easily killed; same as a setup.

Point: Unit of scoring; tally scored by a successful player. Only the server can score a point.

Point of contact: The exact spot at which the racquet strikes the ball.

Power player: A player who relies primarily on hitting the ball hard rather than emphasizing accuracy and/or finesse.

Psych out: To gain a mental edge over an opponent through the use of psychological ploys. To falter mentally and lose a shot or match that should have been a certainty.

Psych up: To prepare mentally before or during a match.

Rally: An exchange of shots after the serve, which is continued until play ends.

Ready position: The stance taken while waiting for a serve or a shot.

Receiver: The player returning serve.

Receiving line: Same as five-foot line.

Referee: The person who makes all judgment calls in tournament play.

Retriever: A player whose specialty is retrieving.

Roll-out: A shot in which the ball rolls out on the floor after rebounding off the front wall. A sure point, since it is impossible to retrieve.

Safety hinder: The interruption of a rally when continued play could cause an injury. The point is replayed.

Screen: Interference with the opponent's vision of the ball.

Serve: The act of putting the ball in play.

Server: Player who puts the ball in play.

Serve return: The shot used to return the served ball.

Service box: The area 1½ feet from the side wall where the nonserving member of a doubles team stands with his/her back to the wall while his/her partner serves. Considered part of service zone during service.

Service line: The front line of the service zone.

Service zone: The court area between the short line and the service line, from side wall to side wall, where the server must stand while serving.

Set position: The ready position or the initial stance assumed by a player about to hit the ball.

Setup: A potential shot during the rally that should be an easy scoring opportunity for the hitter; used synonymously with "plum" term.

Shooter: An aggressive player who adopts an attack strategy; his/her shot selection relies heavily on the kill.

Short line: The back line of the service zone line, which divides court into equal halves.

Short serve: A serve that fails to rebound beyond the short line. This serve is illegal, and two such serves in succession result in loss of service.

Side-by-side formation: A method of player positioning when playing doubles. Each player covers half of the court, either the left or right side. Synonymous with "half-and-half" term.

Side-out: Loss of serve.

Singles: A racquetball game in which one player opposes another player.

Skip ball: A low ball that hits the floor before reaching the front wall.

Southpaw: A left-handed player; "portsider."

Spin: The intended or unintended "English" imparted to the ball by the racquet strings during the stroke.

Stall: To intentionally delay the progress of the game.

Straddle ball: Any shot that passes through the legs of one of the players after the front wall rebound; this is a hinder only if it visually or physically impedes the other player from hitting the ball.

Sweet spot: The area of the racquet face that provides the most control and power; generally the center of the strings.

Target area: The area of the front wall at which a serve or shot is aimed.

Tension: The amount of pressure with which a racquet is strung.

Thong: Strap attached to a racquet and worn around the player's wrist. The strap must be fastened securely to eliminate the possibility of the racquet flying out of control.

Three-wall racquetball: An outdoor variety of the sport in which a front and two partial or full side walls are utilized; the back wall is replaced by a line on the playing surface.

Three-wall serve: An illegal serve that strikes three walls before hitting the floor; serve striking the front wall, side wall and opposite side wall; counts as one service fault.

Throat: The part of the racquet between the strings and the grip.

Tiebreaker: The third game of a match, which is usually played to eleven points.

Time-out: A legal break in play called for by one player or team.

Topspin: Rotation of the ball in a clockwise direction.

Tournament: Formal supervised play in which trophies, prizes or money are often awarded the top finishers.

Trigger grip: Method of holding the racquet as if it were a pistol.

Unavoidable hinder: Accidental interference with an opponent or the flight of the ball. No penalty is suffered, and the rally is replayed.

USRA: United States Racquetball Association; no longer exists.

V shot: A shot whereby the ball hits the front wall, then rebounds off the side wall near the short line. The ball rebounds behind the opponent.

Volley: To hit the ball on the fly before it bounces. This is legal both on the serve return and during the rally. Also called a fly shot.

Wallpaper shot: A shot hit close to the side wall; difficult to return.

Winner: A successful shot that results in a point or side-out.

Z ball: A shot that hits the front wall, a side wall, and then the opposite wall before striking the floor.

Z serve: Same as Z ball, except the ball hits the floor before hitting the third wall.

Racquetball Bibliography and Resource Directory

Books

Allsen, Philip E. and Witbeck, Alan R.: *Racquetball/Paddleball*. Dubuque, Iowa, Wm. C. Brown, 1972.

_____: *Racquetball/Paddleball*, 2nd ed. Dubuque, Iowa, Wm. C. Brown, 1977.

_____: *Racquetball*. Dubuque, Iowa, Wm. C. Brown, 1981.

Boccaccio, Tony: *Racquetball Basics*. Englewood Cliffs, New Jersey, Prentice-Hall, 1979.

Brumfield, Charles and Bairstow, Jeffrey: *Off the Wall*. Pinebrook, New Jersey, Dial Press, 1978.

Darden, Ellington: *Power Racquetball: Featuring PST*. West Point, New York, Leisure Press, 1981.

Dowell, Linus J. and Grice, William A.: *Racquetball*. Boston, American Press, 1979.

Fichter, George S.: *Racquetball*. New York, Watts, 1979.

Fleming, A. William and Bloom, Joel A.: *Paddleball and Racquetball*. Pacific Palisades, California, Goodyear, 1973.

Garfinkel, Charles: *Racquetball the Easy Way*. New York, Atheneum, 1978.

Hogan, Marty and Brumfield, Charles: *Power Racquetball*. Chicago, Contemporary Books, 1978.

Keeley, Steve: *The Complete Book of Racquetball*. Northfield, Illinois, DBI Books, 1976.

Kramer, Jack: *Beginner's Racquetball Book*. Mountain View, California, Anderson World, 1979.

Leve, Charles: *Inside Racquetball*. Chicago, Regnery, 1973.

Lubarsky, Steve et al.: *How to Improve Your Racquetball*. North Hollywood, California, Wilshire, 1980.

_____: *Racquetball Made Easy*. North Hollywood, California, Wilshire, 1978.

Maclean, N.: *Platform Tennis, Racquetball and Paddleball*. Orlando, Florida, Drake, 1977.

Moore, Alan C. et al.: *Racquetball for All*. Dubuque, Iowa, Kendall-Hunt, 1979.

National Association for Girls and Women in Sport: *Team Handball, Racquetball, Orienteering*. Washington, D.C., AAHPER, 1978.

Norton, Cheryl and Bryant, James E.: *Racquetball: A Guide for the Aspiring Player*. Englewood, Colorado, Morton, 1984.

Poynter, Margaret: *The Racquetball Book*. New York, Messner, 1980.

Reznik, John W.: *Racquetball*. New York, Sterling, 1979.

_____: *Racquetball*. New York, Sterling, 1980.

_____ and Peterson, James A. (Ed.): *Championship Racquetball: By the Experts*. West Point, New York, Leisure Press, 1978.

_____ et al.: *Racquetball for Men and Women*. Champaign, Illinois, Stipes, 1972.

Rich, Jim: *Fundamentals of Racquetball*. Dubuque, Iowa, Kendall-Hunt, 1975.

Sauser, Jean and Shay, Arthur: *Beginning Racquetball Drills*. Chicago, Contemporary Books, 1981.

_____: *Inside Racquetball for Women*. Chicago, Contemporary Books, 1977.

_____: *Intermediate Racquetball Drills*. Chicago, Contemporary Books, 1982.

_____: *Racquetball Strategy*. Chicago, Contemporary Books, 1979.

_____: *Teaching Your Child Racquetball*. Chicago, Contemporary Books, 1978.

Scott, Eugene L.: *Racquetball: The Cult*. Garden City, New York, Doubleday, 1979.

Scott, Robert S.: *The Physician and Sportsmedicine Guide to Racquetball and Squash*. New York, McGraw, 1980.

Shay, Arthur and Francher, Terry: *40 Common Errors in Racquetball and How to Correct Them*. Chicago, Contemporary Books, 1979.

_____ and Leve, Charles: *Winning Racquetball*. Chicago, Regnery, 1976.

Sheftel, C. and Shay, Arthur: *Contemporary Racquetball*. Chicago, Contemporary Books, 1978.

Spear, Victor I.: *How to Win at Racquetball*. Chicago, Rand McNally, 1976.

_____: *Sports Illustrated Racquetball*. New York, Lippincott, 1979.

Stafford, Randy: *Racquetball: The Sport for Everyone*. Memphis, S. C. Toof, 1975.

_____: *Racquetball: The Sport for Everyone*, revised edition. Memphis, S. C. Toof, 1982.

_____: *Racquetball: The Sport for Everyone*, 2nd ed., Memphis, Stafford, 1984.

Strandemo, Steve and Bruns, Bill: *Advanced Racquetball*. New York, Pocket Books, 1981.

_____: *The Racquetball Book*. New York, Pocket Books, 1977.

Sylvis, James: *Racquetball for Everyone: Technique and Strategy*. Englewood Cliffs, New Jersey, Prentice-Hall, 1985.

Verner, Bill and Skowrup, Drew: *Racquetball*. Palo Alto, California, Mayfield, 1977.

_____: *Racquetball: Basic Skills and Drills,* 2nd ed., Palo Alto, California, Mayfield, 1985.

Weckstein, Joyce: *Racquetball for Women.* Royal Oak, Michigan, Lincoln Press, 1975.

Wickstrom, Ralph and Larson, Charles: *Racquetball and Paddleball Fundamentals.* Columbus, Ohio, Merrill, 1972.

Wright, Shannon and Keeley, Steve: *The Women's Book of Racquetball.* Chicago, Contemporary Books, 1980.

Periodicals

National Racquetball. Monthly publication of United States Racquetball Association (USRA). Publication Management, Inc., 1980 Pickwick Avenue, Glenview, Illinois 60025.

Racquetball in Review. Monthly publication of American Amateur Racquetball Association (AARA). 815 N. Weber, Colorado Springs, Colorado 80903.

Racquetball Industry. Bi-monthly publication. 1545 N.E. 123rd Street, Suite 2-C, North Miami, Florida 33161.

Selected Periodical Articles on Racquetball Injuries

Ardito, Joe: Should we make eye guards a must? *National Racquetball,* 6:12, 1978.

Buetstein, Richard J.: Heal thyself. *Racquetball.* 10:22-25, 1981.

Carlson, Tom: Playing hurt. *Racquetball,* 8:15-20, 1979.

_____: Wounded knee. *Racquetball,* 8:27-30, 1979.

Della-Guistine, Daniel: Racquetball safety problem. *Athletic Purchasing and Facilities,* 4:40, 1980.

Easterbrook, Michael: Eye injuries in racket sports: A continuing problem. *Physician and Sportsmedicine,* 9:91-94, 97, 100-101, 1981.

_____: Eye protection for squash and racquetball players. *Physician and Sportsmedicine,* 9:79-82, 1981.

_____: Working to save your eyes. *National Racquetball,* 11:6-9, 1982.

Goulart, Frances S.: The aspirin alternative: Racquetball without pain. *National Racquetball,* 9:76-79, 1980.

Kort, Michele: Eye injuries. *Racquetball Illustrated,* 3:58, 60, 1980.

La Bonne, Mike: Eye injuries. *Racquetball,* 9:23-24, 1980.

McDonough, Tom: A little dab will do you. *Racquetball,* 9:21-22, 26, 1980.

Meagher, Jack and Broughton, Pat: Sports massage. *Racquetball Illustrated,* 2:59-61, 1979.

Meyers, Lindsay: Keep your eye on the ball, not the other way around. *National Racquetball,* 9:38-39, 1980.

Miller, Alison: First aid: What you don't know can hurt you. *Racquetball,* 10:22-24, 1981.

Newman, Donna J.: Two ways to cure racquetball elbow: Acupuncture (Part 2). *National Racquetball*, 10:20-21, 1981.

Rose, Clifton P. and Morse, James O.: Racquetball injuries. *Physician and Sportsmedicine*, 7:72-75, 78, 1979.

Scott, Robert: From beans to bursa. *Racquetball Illustrated*, 1:56-58, 1978.

_____: Let's look at eye injuries. *Racquetball Illustrated*, 1:53-54, 1978.

Turley, Susan: How dry I am: It's called dehydration, and it isn't funny. *Racquetball*, 8:21-23, 26, 1979.

Wolf, Clifford Jay: Recognizing foot injuries. *Racquetball Illustrated*, 1:68, 70-71, 1979.

Ziehm, Len: What's being done to decrease eye injuries in racquetball? *Racquetball*, 10:17, 19, 1981.

Selected Periodical Articles on Racquetball Skills Tests

Bartee, Horace and Fothergill, Richard W.: Tests of racquetball skills. *Texas Association for Health, Physical Education and Recreation Journal*, 48:8, 32, 1980.

Collins, Ray and Hodges, Pat: Racquetball skills test investigation. *Minnesota Journal for Health, Physical Education, Recreation and Dance*, 10:10-12, 1982.

Durstine, J. Larry and Drowatsky, John N.: Racquetball success: Skill and more. *Learning and Physical Education Newsletter*, Fall:12, 1979.

Hensley, Larry D., East, Whitfield B. and Stillwell, Jim L.: A racquetball skills test. *Research Quarterly*, 50:114-118, 1979.

Dissertations

Buschner, Craig A.: The Validation of a Racquetball Skills Test for College Men. Doctoral dissertation, Stillwater, Oklahoma State University, 1976.

Grant, Roger H.: The Effects of Subliminally Projected Visual Stimuli on Skill Development, Selected Attention, and Participation in Racquetball by College Students. Doctoral dissertation, Commerce, East Texas State University, 1980.

Grice, William A.: An Analysis of Exercise Intensity, Glucose and Lactic Acid Concentration, and Heart Rate Response in Selected College Male Racquetball Players During Competition. Doctoral dissertation, Natchitoches, Northwestern State University of Louisiana, 1980.

Klass, Robert A.: The Validation of a Battery of Reaction Time Tests to Predict Racquetball Ability for College Men. Doctoral dissertation, Stillwater, Oklahoma State University, 1977.

Shemwell, James A., Jr.: Validation of the James-Lowell Racquetball Test: A Skills and Ability Test for Use in Instructional Racquetball. Doctoral dissertation, Murfreesboro, Middle Tennessee State University, 1980.

Theses

Dennis, David C.: Racquetball Skill Level and Maximal Oxygen Uptake. Master's thesis, Fullerton, California State University, 1979.

Epperson, Steve: Validation of the Reznik Racquetball Test. Master's thesis, Pullman, Washington State University, 1977.

Other Instructional Materials

Keeley, Steve: *Racquetball Lessons Made Easy*, MacDonald Associates. (two one-hour instructional cassettes and booklet)

_____: *It's a Racquet!*, Haslett, Michigan, Service Press. (racquetball anecdote book)

_____: *The Kill and Rekill Gang*, Haslett, Michigan, Service Press. (racquetball cartoon book)

_____: *Racquetball 103-Beginners, and Racquetball 203-Advanced*, Strokeminder. (three replay flipbooks and course material)

Muehleisen, Bud: *Dr. Bud Muehleisen on Racquetball*, San Diego, Video-Sports, Inc. (twenty-five minute videocassette)

Racquetball Organizations

AMERICAN AMATEUR RACQUETBALL ASSOCIATION (AARA)
815 N. Weber
Colorado Springs, Colorado 80903

Promotes racquetball as a sport; organizes racquetball to be a self-governing sport of, by and for the players; encourages building facilities for the sport; conducts racquetball events including annual national tournaments; recognized by the United States Olympic Committee as the official ruling body of racquetball; formerly International Racquetball Association.

AMERICAN RACQUETBALL HANDICAP SYSTEM (ARHS)
10237 Yellow Circle Drive
Minnetonka, Minnesota 55343

Provides objective player performance ratings for racquetball players of all ability levels; official ranking service for the American Amateur Racquetball Association.

AMERICAN PROFESSIONAL RACQUETBALL ORGANIZATION (APRO)
730 Pine
Deerfield, Illinois 60015

Racquetball's equivalent to the United States Professional Tennis Association (USPTA).

INTERNATIONAL AMATEUR RACQUETBALL FEDERATION (IARF)
815 N. Weber
Colorado Springs, Colorado 80903

International racquetball organization that catered mainly to amateur players; now the American Amateur Racquetball Association (AARA).

NATIONAL LEFT-HANDERS RACQUET SPORTS ASSOCIATION (NLHRSA)

3042 Rosa DelVilla
Gulf Breeze, Florida 32561

Assists left-handers in using their left-handedness to better advantage in racquet sports.

NATIONAL RACQUETBALL CLINICS, INC.

10251 Scripps Ranch Road
San Diego, California 92123

Group of top names in racquetball offering clinics and exhibitions.

OHIO RACQUETBALL ASSOCIATION (ORA)

127 Northfield Road
Bedford, Ohio 44146

Example of a state organization that acts as a coordinating body for tournaments, clinics, etc.

UNITED RACQUET SPORTS FOR WOMEN (URW)

P.O. Box 230
New York, New York 10461

Represents women's interests in all racquet sports.

WOMEN'S PROFESSIONAL RACQUETBALL ASSOCIATION (WPRA)

3727 Centennial Circle
Las Vegas, Nevada 89121

The racquetball organization for professional women players.

Suppliers of Racquetball Products

AMF HEAD

Box CN-5227
Princeton, NJ 08540

BALL HOPPER PRODUCTS, INC.

3026 Commercial Avenue
Northbrook, Illinois 60062

CARRERA

P.O. Box 2
Norwood, New Jersey 07648

COURT PRODUCTS, INC.

1500 Deerfield Road
Highland Park, Illinois 60035

DIVERSIFIED PRODUCTS

309 Williamson Avenue
Opelika, Alabama 36802

EKTELON

8929 Aero Drive
San Diego, California 92123

FOOT-JOY, INC.
144 Field Street
Brockton, Massachusetts 02403

HOGAN RACQUETBALL
7444 Trade Street
San Diego, California 92121

HOLLMAN COURT SYSTEM
11200 S.W. Allen Avenue
Beaverton, Oregon 97005

LLOYD DISTRIBUTORS, INC.
P.O. Box 3000
Calabasas, California 91302

M-M COURT SYSTEMS, INC.
2160 Fletcher Parkway, Suite-J
El Cajon, California 92020

OLYMPIAN RACQUETBALL
5567 Kearny Villa Road
San Diego, California 92123

OMEGA SPORTS
9200 Cody
Overland Park, Kansas 66212

PENN ATHLETIC PRODUCTS COMPANY
3065 45th Avenue
Phoenix, Arizona 85043

SARANAC GLOVE COMPANY
P.O. Box 786
Green Bay, Wisconsin 54305

SEAMCO, INC.
Hatfield, Pennsylvania 19440

SLAZENGER, INC.
Box 160
Cornwells Heights, Pennsylvania 19020

SPORTS PAL COMPANY, INC.
P.O. Box 28906
St. Louis, Missouri 63132

SPORTS UNLIMITED
P.O. Box 1207
Stillwater, Oklahoma 74074

VOIT, INC.
5741 Rostrata Avenue
Buena Park, California 90621

WILSON SPORTING GOODS

8950 W. Palmer Street
River Grove, Illinois 60171

WORLD COURTS, INC.

554 Main Street, Dept. A
S. Weymouth, Massachusetts 02190

American Racquetball Handicap System*

BACKGROUND AND PHILOSOPHY

The American Racquetball Handicap System (ARHS) was founded in 1982 in Minnetonka, Minnesota for the purpose of providing objective player performance ratings for players of all levels in the sport of racquetball. Today, ARHS is a national system operating in clubs throughout the country.

Prior to ARHS, player performance ratings in racquetball were unearned, self-declared comfort levels such as A, B, C and Novice. Players did not earn these ratings but merely selected them based on how they viewed their ability. The inherent problem of the self-declared system is that the categories (A, B, C, etc.) are too broad, leading to the false assumption that all players in a particular category are near the same ability.

When these self-declared player ratings are used to program events such as leagues and tournaments, the subjective nature of the system provides players the opportunity to consciously or unconsciously "sandbag" (underrate their ability). The resulting mismatches are generally uncomfortable experiences for both players.

The concept of players earning their performance ratings is not new. For example, when a golfer states that he or she is a 12-handicap, this is not a rating that is arbitrarily selected; rather it is a performance rating that the player has earned through the results of playing the game and turning in his or her scores for entry into the handicap (rating) system.

Fundamentally, ARHS is a results-oriented, player performance rating system. Actual game scores are processed by computer through a mathematical formula, and player ratings are adjusted according to these results. The methodology is based on the theory that whenever two rated players compete, based on the difference in their ratings, there is an expected outcome or point spread. The computer then compares this expected point spread with the actual results or point spread of the game, and then adjusts the ratings of the two opponents accordingly. With this system, players do not always have to win to show an improvement in their rating. Example:

John has a rating of 545

Bob has a rating of 500

John and Bob play a game to 21 and John wins 21 to 19 and turns in the score to ARHS. With a rating difference of 45, the system predicts that in a game to 21, the expected point spread (game handicap) is 4, or John should beat Bob by 4 or more points. Since John beat Bob by 2 points (21-19) in the actual game, John's rating would go down and Bob's rating would improve.

ARHS ratings add the element of playing against yourself to improve your rating as well as playing against your opponent. Instead of the traditional "winner take all'' method of rewarding a player, in this example there are actually two winners, John, who won the game, and Bob, whose rating improved.

HOW IT WORKS IN CLUBS

The first thing a player does to enroll in the system is to fill out a player information form. This form requests some basic demographic information as well as having the player rate his or her racquetball game on a scale from 1 to 10 (Novice through high A). It also asks for the player's playing preference (day of week and time of day). Once a player has filled out an information form, he or she can then start recording the scores of his or her competitive matches. Although it is not necessary for a player to turn in the results of all of his or her matches, he or she is encouraged to submit league and tournament games, as well as competitive recreational games.

Score card signs are located throughout the club, making it convenient for players to record their scores. The completed score cards are then sent to ARHS.

Initially, the player's self-declared evaluation on the information form becomes a three-digit rating in the system. For example, if a player indicated that he or she was a middle B, the individual would be assigned an ARHS rating of 520.

Player ratings are updated twice a month and posted on the club's roster report. New players in the system have an asterisk in front of their rating which simply means that they have not turned in 18 games or more; therefore, their rating possibly reflects their self-declared evaluation rather than their earned rating. After 18 games, the asterisk is removed and the player has an earned rating.

Also found on the roster is the player's ranking within the club. The player with the highest rating is ranked number one. In addition, the roster report includes the player's previous rating as well as how many games he or she currently has entered into the system. Next is the coding of the player's preference for time of the day and day of the week he or she likes to play racquetball. The player's home and business phone numbers and occupation also are recorded.

The club roster helps players find competitive, compatible matches. It provides them with information on how good a player is, how often and when he or she likes to play, and how to get in touch with him or her. This information goes far beyond the old type of club roster that only reported whether an individual was an A, B, or C player.

In addition to the club roster, match results are posted twice a month. This is a list of results of all matches occurring during the current rating period.

Four times per year each player receives his or her ARHS I.D. card and evaluation report. This report analyzes the player's racquetball games over the previous three months, reporting the person's win/loss record, the average rating of the opponents, his or her success against the expected outcome (game handicap), and his or her rating change for the period. This statistical evaluation motivates players to be more mentally involved in their racquetball game.

ARHS ratings help clubs set up their racquetball programs and events. When players sign up for leagues and tournaments, their current ARHS rating determines what performance division they play in. This significantly reduces sandbagging and helps keep competition more evenly matched.

With ARHS ratings, clubs also have a method to handicap games and matches. When matches in leagues, tournaments or challenge courts are handicapped, the winner is the player that beats the expected outcome (game handicap), which may or may not be the player that attains the most points.

Because ARHS is for players at all levels, the system recognizes players for active participation rather than just for winning. For example, on the Player of the Month Plaque that hangs in each club, there are the names of the monthly winners in three categories: (1) Most Games Played; (2) Most Rating Improvement; (3) Best Against the Handicap. Each monthly winner receives a "You Rate With Us!" tee shirt and the recognition within his or her club.

There is also the Monthly Achievers Club which each month lists the players that show an improvement in their ARHS rating (5-15 points Bronze achievers; 16-25 points Silver achievers; over 25 points Gold achievers). Each of these computerized programs recognize players for their competitive participation.

The ARHS rating system provides racquetball with a standardized method of measuring player performance throughout the sport. It links all of racquetball into a common program that players of all ability levels can use and enjoy.

---

*Patrick J. McGlone, president of the American Racquetball Handicap System, 10237 Yellow Circle Drive, Minnetonka, Minnesota 55343.

Appendix

OFFICIAL RACQUETBALL RULES AND REGULATIONS*

The following rule changes were approved by the AARA Board of Directors and will go into effect September 1, 1985.

Rule 2.A. Order

The player or team winning the coin toss has the option to serve or receive for the start of the first game. The second game will begin in reverse order of the first game. The player or team scoring the highest total of points in Games 1 and 2 will have the option to serve or receive for the start of the tiebreaker. In the event that both players or teams score an equal number of points in the first two games, another coin toss will take place and the winner of the toss will have the option to serve or receive.

Rule 13.D. Between Games

The rest period between the first two games of a match is two minutes. If a tiebreaker is necessary, the rest period between the second and third game is five minutes.

Rule 7.H. Out-Of-Order Serve

In doubles, when either partner serves out-of-order the points scored by that server will be subtracted and an out serve will be called: if the second server serves out-of-order the out serve will be applied to the first server and the second server will resume serving. If the player designated as the first server serves out-of-order, a sideout will be called. In a match with line judges, the referee may enlist their aid to recall the number of points scored out-of-order.

2 — COURTS AND EQUIPMENT

A. COURTS

    e) Receiving Line. A broken line parallel with and five feet to the rear of the short line. The receiving line will begin with a line 21 inches long that extends from each side wall: the two lines will be connected by an alternate series of six-inch spaces and six-inch lines (17 six-inch spaces and 16 six-inch lines). The back edge of the receiving line will be five-feet from the back edge of the short line. IMPORTANT NOTE: Sites of all state, regional and national championships taking place after Sept. 1, 1985 must have the receiving line painted on the floor. Until Sept. 1, 1986, all other sanctioned tournaments may use tape to designate the receiving line. Official court specifications must be complied with by Sept. 1, 1986.

D. RACQUET SPECIFICATIONS

    l) Dimensions. (Current language)
       IMPORTANT NOTE: For a one-year period beginning Sept. 1, 1985, the above racquet dimensions have been waived for experimental purposes. For that period, the lone specification is that the racquet, including bumper guard and all solid parts, may not exceed 21 inches in length.

1 — THE GAME

A. TYPES OF GAMES
Racquetball may be played by two, three, or four players. When played by two it is called "singles", when played by three "cutthroat", and when played by four, "doubles."

B. DESCRIPTION
Racquetball, as the name implies, is a competitive game in which only one racquet is used by each player to serve and return the ball.

C. OBJECTIVE
The objective is to win each rally by serving or returning the ball so the opponent is unable to keep the ball in play. A rally is over when a side makes an error, or is unable to return the ball before it touches the floor twice, or if a hinder is called.

D. POINTS AND OUTS
Points are scored only by the server (serving team) when it serves an ace or wins a rally. When the serving side loses a rally, it loses the serve. Losing the serve is called an "out" in singles, and a "hand out" or "side out" in doubles.

E. GAME
A game is won by the side first scoring 15 points. The third game, referred to as the tiebreaker, is played to 11. It is necessary to win only by one point.

F. MATCH
A match is won by the first side winning two games. The first two games of a match are played to 15 points. In the event each side wins one game, the match shall be decided by an 11-point tiebreaker.

G. DOUBLES TEAM
A doubles team shall consist of two players that meet either/or the age requirements or player classification requirements to participate in a particular division of play. A team must be classified by the ability level (or player classification) of the higher ranked player on the team.

A change in playing partners may not be made after the final draw has been made and posted. Under no circumstances can a partner change be made during the course of a tournament without the consent of the Tournament Director.

H. CONSOLATION MATCHES
1) Consolation matches may be waived at the discretion of the Tournament Director, but this waiver must be in writing on the tournament application.
2) In all AARA sanctioned tournaments each entrant shall be entitled to participate in a minimum of two matches. This then means that losers of their first match shall have the opportunity to compete in a consolation bracket of their own division. In draws of less than seven players, a round robin format may be offered.
3) Preliminary matches will be two of three games to 11 points. Semifinals and finals matches will follow the regular scoring format.

2 — COURTS AND EQUIPMENT

A. COURTS
The specifications for the standard four wall racquetball court are:
1) **Dimension:** The dimensions shall be 20 feet wide, 20 feet high, and 40 feet long, with a back wall at least 12 feet high. All surfaces within the court shall be deemed "in play" with the exception of any gallery openings or surfaces designated as "court-hinders."
2) **Lines and Zones** Racquetball courts shall be divided and marked with 1½ inch wide lines as follows:
   a) **Short Line.** The back edge of the short line is midway between (20') and parallel to the front and back walls, thus dividing the court into equal front and back courts.
   b) **Service Line.** The front edge of the service line is parallel with and located five feet in front of the back edge of the short line.
   c) **Service Zone.** The service zone is the area between the outer edges of the short and service lines.
   d) **Services Boxes.** The service boxes are located at each end of the service zone and designated by lines parallel with each side wall. The inside edge of the lines are 18 inches from the side walls.
   e) **Receiving Line.** Five feet back of the short line, vertical lines shall be marked on each side wall extending three to six inches from the floor. The back edge of the receiving lines shall be five feet from the back edge of the short line.
   IMPORTANT NOTE: The following receiving line is recommended for adoption, effective September 1, 1986: Receiving Lines. A non-solid line five feet back of the short line. The receiving line is designated on the court floor by 21-inch lines parrallel to the front wall, that extend from each side wall and are connected by a series of six-inch lines separated by six-inch spaces (16 six-inch lines and 17 six-inch spaces). The back edge of the receiving lines shall be five feet from the back edge of the short line.

f) **Safety Zone.** The five-foot area bounded by the short line and the receiving line. The zone is observed only during the serve. Entering the zone prematurely: 1) if the receiver commits the infraction, it results in a point; 2) if the server commits the infraction, it results in the loss of serve. (See 3.8.A. and 3.7.I.)

B. BALL SPECIFICATIONS

1) The standard racquetball shall be 2¼" in diameter; weigh approximately 1.4 ounces, and at a temperature of 70-74 degrees F., with a 100 inch drop rebound is to be 68-72 inches; hardness, 55-60 inches durometer.
2) Any ball which carried the endorsement of approval from the AARA is an official ball. Only AARA approved balls may be used in AARA sanctioned tournaments.

C. BALL SELECTION

1) A ball shall be selected by the referee for use in each match. During the match, the referee either at his discretion, or at the request of a player or team, may replace the game ball. Balls that are not round or which bounce erratically shall not be used.
2) In tournament play, the referee and the players shall agree to an alternate ball, so that in the event of breakage, the second ball can be put into play immediately.

D. RACQUET SPECIFICATIONS

1) **Dimensions.** The total length and width of the racquet may not exceed 27 inches. The length of the racquet may not exceed 20½ inches and the head width may not exceed nine inches. These measurements are computed from the outer edge of the rims, not including bumper guard, and from the farthest solid part of the handle.
2) The regulation racquet frame may be of any material, as long as it conforms to the above specifications.
3) The regulation racquet frame must include a thong that must be securely attached to the player's wrist.
4) The string of the racquet should be gut, monofilament, nylon, graphite, plastic, metal, or a combination thereof, providing strings do not mark or deface the ball.

E. UNIFORM

1) The uniform and shoes may be of any color,but the shoes must have soles which do not mark or damage the court floor. The shirt may contain any insignia or writing considered in good taste by the Tournament Director. Players are required to wear shirts. Extremely loose fitting or otherwise distracting garments are not permissable.
2) Eye protection is required for any participant under the age of 19 in all AARA sanctioned tournaments.

3 — OFFICIATING AND PLAY REGULATIONS

Rule 1. A. Tournaments
All tournaments shall be managed by a committee or Tournament Director who shall designate the officials.

Rule. 1. B. Officials
The official shall be a referee designated by the Tournament Director or the floor manager or one agreed to by both participants (teams in doubles). Officials may also include, at the discretion of the tournament director, a scorekeeper and two linespeople.

Rule 1. C. Removal of Referee
A referee may be removed upon the agreement of both participants (teams in doubles) or at the discretion of the Tournament Director or rules officials. In the event that a referee's removal is requested by one player (team) and not agreed to by the other, the Tournament Director or officials may accept or reject the request.

Rule 1. D. Rule Briefing
Before all tournaments, all officials and players shall be briefed on rules and on court hinders or regulations or modifications the Tournament Director wishes to impose. The briefing should be reduced to writing. The current AARA rules will apply and be made available. Any modifications the Tournament Director wishes to impose must be stated on the entry form and in writing and be available to all players at registration.

Rule 1. E. Referees
1) **Pre-match duties.** Before each match begins, it shall be the duty of the referee to:
   a) Check on adequacy of preparation of court with respect to cleanliness, lighting, and temperature;
   b) Check on availability and suitability of materials - to include balls, towels, scorecards, pencils, and timepiece - necessary for the match;
   c) Go on court to instruct players;
   d) Point out court hinders and note any local regulations;
   e) Inspect equipment and toss coin;
   f) Check linespeople and scorekeeper and ask for reserve game ball upon assuming officiating position;

110

g) Review any rule modifications in effect for this particular tournament.

2) **Decisions.** During the match, the referee shall make all decisions with regard to the rules. Where linespeople are used, the referee shall announce all final judgments. If both players in singles and three out of four in a doubles match disagree with a judgment call made by the referee, the referee is overruled. The referee shall have jurisdiction over the spectators as well as players while the match is in progress.

3) **Protests.** Any decision not involving the judgment of the referee may, on protest, be decided by the Tournament Director or designated official.

4) **Forfeitures.** A match may be forfeited by the referee when:
   a) Any player refuses to abide by the referee's decision, or engages in unsportsmanlike conduct;
   b) A player or team may be forfeited by the Tournament Director or official for failure to comply with the tournament or host facility's rules while on the premises, for failure to referee, for improper conduct on the premises between matches, or for abuse of hospitality, locker room, or other rules and procedures.
   c) Any player or team who fails to report to play 10 minutes after the match has been scheduled to play. (The Tournament Director may permit a longer delay if circumstances warrant such a decision.)

5) **Other Rulings.** The referee may rule on all matters not covered in the AARA Official Rules. However, the referee may be overruled by the Tournament Director.

Rule 1. F. 1) Linespeople

Two linespeople are recommended for all matches from the semifinals on up, subject to availability and subject to the discretion of the tournament officials. The linespeople shall be selected by the officials and situated as designated by the officials. If any player objects to the selection of a linesperson before the match begins, all reasonable effort shall be made to find a replacement acceptable to the officials and players. If a player or team objects to a linesperson after the match begins, replacement shall be under the discretion of the referee and officials.

Rule 1. F. 2) Linespeople

Linespeople are designated in order to help decide appealed rulings. Two linespeople will be designated by the referee and shall, at the referee's signal, either agree or disagree with the referee's ruling. The signal by a linesperson to show agreement with the referee is "thumbs up". The signal to show disagreement is "thumbs down." The signal for no opinion is "open palm down."

If both linespeople signal no opinion, the referee's call stands. If both linespeople disagree with the referee, the referee must reverse the ruling. If one linesperson agrees and one disagrees or has no opinion, the referee's call shall stand. If one linesperson disagrees and one has no opinion, rally or serve shall be replayed. Any replays will result in two serves with the exception of appeals on the second serve itself.

Rule 1. G. Appeals

In any match using line judges a player or team may appeal only the following calls or non-calls by the referee: killshots and skip balls; fault serves; out serves; double-bounce pickups; receiving line violations; rule interpretations.

The appeal must be directed to the referee, who then will request opinions simultaneously from the two line judges. Any appeal made directly to line judges by a player or team or made after an excessive demonstration or complaint by the player(s) will be considered void and any appeal rights for that side for that particular rally will be forfeited.

1) **Kill Shot Appeals.** If the referee makes a call of "good" on a kill shot attempt which ends a particular rally, the loser of the rally may appeal the call. If the appeal is successful and the referee's original call reversed, the side which originally lost the rally is declared the winner of the rally. If the referee makes the call of "bad" or "skip" on a kill shot attempt, the rally has ended and the side against whom the call was made has the right to appeal the call if they felt the shot was good. If the appeal is successful and the referee's original call reversed, the referee must then decide if the shot could have been returned had play continued. If the shot could have been or was (returned), the rally shall be replayed. If the shot was a kill or pass that the opponent could not have retrieved (in the referee's opinion), the side which originally lost the rally is declared the winner of the rally. The referee's judgment in this matter is final. Any rally replayed shall afford the server two serves.

2) **Fault Serve Appeals.** If the referee makes a call of "fault" on a serve, the server may appeal the call. If the appeal is successful, the server is entitled to replay the serve. If the served ball was considered by the referee to be an ace, then a point shall be awarded to the server. If the referee makes "no call" on a serve (therefore indicating that the serve was "good"), either side may appeal, then the situation reverts to the point of service with the call becoming fault. If it was a first service, one more serve is allowed. If the serve was a second serve, then the fault serve would cause an out.

3) **Out Serve Appeals.** If the referee makes a call of "out serve" thereby stopping play, the serving side may appeal the call. If the appeal is successful, the referee shall revise the call to the proper call and the service shall be replayed, or a point awarded if the resulting serve was an ace. If the referee makes "no call", or calls a fault serve, and the receiver feels it was an out serve, the receiver may appeal. If the appeal is successful, the serve service results in an out. Note: A safety zone violation by the server is an out serve.

4) **Double-Bounce Pickup Appeals.** If the referee makes a call of "two bounces", thereby stopping play, the side against whom the call was made has the right of appeal. If the appeal is upheld, the rally is replayed or the referee may award the rally to the hitter if the resulting shot could not have been retrieved by the opponent (and providing the referee's call did not cause the opponent to hesitate or stop play). If the referee makes "no call" on a particular play, indicating thereby that the player hit the ball before the second bounce, the opponent has a right to appeal at the end of the rally. However, since the ball is in play, the side wishing to appeal must clearly motion to the referee and linespeople by raising their non-racquet hand, thereby alerting the officials as to the exact shot which is being appealed. At the same time, the player appealing must continue to play. If the appealing player should lose the rally, and the appeal is upheld, the player who appealed then becomes the winner of the rally. All rallies replayed as the result of a double bounce pickup appeal shall result in the server getting two serves.

5) **Receiving Line (Encroachment) Violation Appeals.** If the referee makes a call of encroachment thereby stopping the play, the receiving side may appeal the call. If the appeal is successful, the service shall be replayed. If the referee makes no call and the server feels there was encroachment, the server may appeal. If the appeal is successful the service results in a point. (For safety zone violation by server or doubles partner, see 1. G. 3).

6) **Rules Interpretations.** If a player feels that the referee has interpreted the rules incorrectly, the player may require the referee or Tournament Director to show him the applicable rule in the rule book.

Rule 2. SERVE

Rule 2. A. Order
The player or side winning the toss becomes the first server and starts the first game. The loser of the toss will serve first in the second game. The player or team scoring the most total points in games one and two shall serve first in the tiebreaker. In the event that both players or teams score an equal number of points in the first two games, another coin toss shall determine the server in the tiebreaker.

RULE 2. B. Start
The serve is started from any place within the service zone. No part of either foot may extend beyond either line of the service zone. Stepping on, but not over the line is permitted. The server must remain in the service zone from the moment the service motion begins until the served ball passes the short line. Violations are called "Foot Faults." The server may not start any service motion until the referee has called the score or the second serve.

Rule 2. C. Manner
Once the service motion begins the ball is dropped or thrown to the floor while standing within the confines of the service zone and, on the first bounce is struck by the racquet so that the ball hits the front wall first and on rebound hits the floor behind the back edge of the short line, either with or without touching one of the side walls. A balk serve or fake swing at the ball shall be deemed an infraction and be judged an out serve.

Rule 2. D. Readiness
Serves shall not be made until the receiving side is ready and the referee has called the score. The referee shall call the score as both serve and receiver prepare to return to their respective position, shortly after the previous point has ended.

Rule 2. E. Delays
Delays on the part of the server or receiver exceeding 10 seconds shall result in an out or point against the offender.

1) The 10-second rule is applicable to the server and receiver simultaneously. Collectively, they are allowed up to 10 seconds, after the score is called, to serve or be ready to receive. It is the server's responsibility to look and be certain the receiver is ready. If the receiver is not ready, he must signal so by raising his racquet above his head or completely turning his back to the server. (These are the only two acceptable signals.)

2) If the server serves the ball while the receiver is signaling "not ready", the serve shall go over with no penalty and the server shall be warned by the referee to check the receiver. If the server continues to serve without checking the receiver, the referee may award a technical for delay of the game.

3) After the score is called, if the server looks at the receiver and the receiver is not signaling "not ready", the server may then serve. If the receiver attempts to signal "not ready" after that point, such signal shall not be acknowledged and the serve becomes legal.

Rule 3. SERVE IN DOUBLES

Rule 3. A. Server
At the beginning of each game in doubles, each side shall inform the referee of the order of service which shall be followed throughout the game. When the first server is out the first time up, the side is out. Thereafter both players on each side shall serve until each receive a handout.

Rule 3. B. Partner's Position
On each serve, the server's partner shall stand erect with back to the sidewall and with both feet on the floor within the service box from the moment the server begins his service motion until the served ball passes the short line. Violations are called "foot faults."

Rule 4. DEFECTIVE SERVES
Defective serves are of three types resulting in penalties as follows:

Rule 4. A. Dead Ball Serve
A dead ball serve results in no penalty and the server is given another serve (without canceling a prior illegal serve.)

Rule 4. B. Fault Serve
Two fault serves result in a handout.

Rule 4. C. Out Serve
An out serve results in a handout.

Rule 5. DEAD BALL SERVES
Dead ball serves do not cancel any previous illegal serve . They occur when an otherwise legal serve:

Rule 5. A. Hits Partner
Hits the server's partner on the fly on the rebound from the front wall while the server's partner is in the service box. Any serve that touches the floor before hitting the partner in the box is short;

Rule 5. B. Screen Balls
Passes so close to the server or server's partner as to obstruct the view of the returning side. Any serve passing behind the server's partner and the side wall is an automatic screen;

Rule 5. C. Court Hinders
Hits any part of the court that under local rules is a dead ball;

Rule 5. D. Broken Ball
If the ball is determined to have broken on the serve, a new ball shall be substituted and the serve shall be replayed (not canceling any prior fault serve).

Rule 6. FAULT SERVES
The following serves are faults and any two in succession result in an out:

Rule 6. A. Foot Faults
A foot fault results when:
1) The server does not begin the service motion with both feet in the service zone;
2) The server steps over the front service line before the served ball passes the short line;
3) In doubles, the server's partner is not in the service box with both feet on the floor and back to the wall from the time the server begins the service motion until the ball passes the short line. If the server, or doubles partner, enters into the safety zone before the served ball passes the short line, it shall result in the loss of serve.

Rule 6. B. Short Service
A short serve is any served ball that first hits the front wall and on the rebound hits the floor on or in front of the short line (with or without touching a side wall);

Rule 6. C. Three-Wall Serve
Any served ball that first hits the front wall and on the rebound hits the two side walls on the fly;

Rule 6. D. Ceiling Serve
Any served ball that first hits the front wall and then touches the ceiling (with or without touching a side wall);

Rule 6. E. Long Serve
Any served ball that first hits the front wall and rebounds to the back wall before touching the floor (with or without touching a side wall);

Rule 6. F. Out-Of-Court Serve
Any served ball that first hits the front wall and, before striking the floor, goes out of the court.

Rule 7. OUT SERVES
Any of the following serves results in an out:

Rule 7. A. Failure of Server
Failure of server to put the ball into play within 10 seconds of the calling of the score by the referee;

Rule 7. B. Missed Ball
Any attempt to strike the ball that results in a total miss or in touching any part of the server's body;

Rule 7. C. Non-Front Serve
Any served ball that does not strike the front wall first;

Rule 7. D. Touched Serve
Any served ball that on the rebound from the front wall touches the server (or server's racquet) or any ball intentionally stopped or caught by the server or server's partner;

Rule 7. E. Crotch Serve
If the served ball hits the crotch of the front wall and floor, front wall and side wall, or front wall and ceiling, it is considered "no good" and is an out serve. A serve into the crotch of the back wall and the floor is good and in play. A served ball hitting the crotch of the side wall and floor (as in a "z" serve) beyond the short line is "good" and in play.

113

Rule 7. F. Illegal Hit

Any illegal hit (contacting the ball twice, carries, or hitting the ball with the handle of the racquet or part of the body or uniform) results in an out serve;

Rule 7. G. Fake or Balk Serve

Such a serve is defined as a non-continuous movement of the racquet towards the ball as the server drops the ball for the purpose of serving and results in an out serve;

Rule 7. H. Out-Of-Order Serve

In doubles, if it is discovered that the second server served first (and is still serving), the penalty shall be that the first server loses his serve. The second server may finish the inning and all points scored will count. If while the first server is serving it is discovered that the second server served first, the penalty shall be an immediate side out. All points served will count. If it is discovered that the first server served, the second server served, and the first server is serving again, the penalty shall be assessment of a technical and all points scored during the first server's extra inning shall be subtracted from their team;

Rule 7. I. Safety Zone Violation

If the server, or doubles partner, enters into the safety zone before the served ball passes the short line, it shall result in the loss of serve.

RULE 8. RETURN OF SERVE

Rule 8. A. Receiving Position

1) The receiver may not enter the safety zone until the ball bounces.
2) On the fly return attempt, the receiver may not strike the ball until the ball breaks the plane of the receiving (5-foot) line. The follow-through may carry the receiver or his racquet past the receiving line.
3) Neither the receiver nor his racquet may break the plane of the short line during the service return.

Any violation by the receiver results in a point for the server.

Rule 8. B. Defective Serve

The receiving side shall not catch or touch a defectively served ball until a call by the referee has been made or it has touched the floor for the second time;

Rule 8. C. Legal Return

After the ball is legally served, one of the players on the receiving side must strike the ball with the racquet either on the fly or after the first bounce and before the ball touches the floor the second time to return the ball to the front wall, either directly or after touching one or both side walls, the back wall or the ceiling, or any combination of those surfaces. A returned ball may not touch the floor before touching the front wall;

Rule 8. D. Failure To Return

The failure to return a serve results in a point for the server.

RULE 9. CHANGES OF SERVE

Rule 9. A. Outs

A server is entitled to continue serving until:

1) **Out Serve.** The player commits an out serve as per rule 7;
2) Player commits two fault serves in succession as per rule 6;
3) **Hits Partner.** Player hits their partner with an attempted return;
4) **Return Failure.** Player or partner fails to hit the ball on one bounce or fails to return the ball to the front wall on a fly (with or without hitting any combination of walls and ceiling);
5) **Avoidable Hinder.** Player or partner commits an avoidable hinder as per rule 12.

Rule 9. B. Side out

In singles, a single handout or out, equals a side out and retires the server. In doubles, a single handout equals a side out on the first service of each game; thereafter, two handouts equal a side out and thereby retires the serving team.

Rule 9. C. Effect

When the server, or the serving team, receives a side out, the server(s) become(s) the receiver(s) and the receiver(s) become(s) the server(s).

RULE 10. RALLIES

Each legal return after the serve is called a rally. Play during rallies shall be according to the following rules:

Rule 10. A. Legal Hits

Only the head of the racquet may be used at any time to return the ball. The racquet may be held in one or both hands. Switching hands to hit a ball, touching the ball with any part of the body or uniform, or removing the wrist thong result in loss of the rally;

Rule 10. B. One Touch

In attempting returns, the ball may be touched or struck only once by a player or team or the result is a loss of rally. The ball may not be "carried." (A carried ball is one which rests on the racquet in such a way that the effect is more of a "sling" or "throw" than a hit.)

Rule 10. C. Failure to Return
Any of the following constitutes a failure to make a legal return during a rally:
1) The ball bounces on the floor more than once before being hit;
2) The ball does not reach the front wall on the fly;
3) The ball caroms off a player's racquet into a gallery or wall opening without first hitting the front wall;
4) A ball which obviously did not have the velocity or direction to hit the front wall strikes another player on the court;
5) A ball struck by one player on a team hits that player's partner, or a player is struck by a ball which was previously hit by that player, or partner;
6) An avoidable hinder as per rule 12 is committed.

Rule 10. D. Effect
Violations of Rule 10.A.,B., and C. result in a loss of rally. If the serving player or team loses the rally, it is an "out" (handout or side out). If the receiver(s) loses the rally, it results in a point for the server(s).

Rule 10. E. Return Attempts
1) In singles, if a player swings at, but misses the ball, the player may continue to attempt to return the ball until it touches the floor for the second time.
2) In doubles, if one player swings at, but misses the ball, both partners may make further attempts to return the ball until it touches the floor the second time. Both partners on a side are entitled to return the ball.

Rule 10. F. Out-Of-Court Ball
1) **After Return.** Any ball returned to the front wall which on the rebound or the first bounce goes into the gallery or through any opening in a sidewall shall be declared dead and the server shall receive two serves.
2) **No Return.** Any ball not returned to the front wall, but which caroms off a player's racquet into the gallery or into any opening in a sidewall either with or without touching the ceiling, side, or back wall, shall be an out or point against the player(s) failing to make the return.

Rule 10. H. Broken Ball
If there is any suspicion that a ball has broken on the serve, or during a rally, play shall continue until the end of the rally. The referee or any player may request the ball be examined. If the referee decides the ball is broken, a new ball shall be put into play and the server given two serves. The only proper way to check for a broken ball is to squeeze it by hand. (Checking the ball by striking it with a racquet will not be considered a valid check and shall work to the disadvantage of the player or team which struck the ball after the rally.)

Rule 10. I. Play Stoppage
If a player loses a shoe or other equipment, or foreign objects enter the court, or any outside interference occurs, the referee shall stop the play if such occurance interfers with ensuing play or player's safety.

Rule 10. J. Replays
Any rallies which are replayed for any reason without the awarding of a point or side out shall result in any previous faults being canceled and the server awarded two serves.

RULE 11. DEAD BALL HINDERS
Dead ball hinders result in the rally being replayed without penalty and the server receiving two serves.

Rule 11. A. Situations
1) **Court hinders.** A ball that hits any part of the court which has been designated is a court hinder, or any ball that takes an irregular bounce off a rough or irregular surface in such a manner as the referee determines that said irregular bounce affected the rally.
2) **Hitting opponent.** Any returned ball that touches an opponent on the fly before it returns to the front wall. The player that has been hit or "nicked" by the ball may make this call, but it must be made immediately and acknowledged by the referee. Any ball which hits an opponent that obviously did not have the velocity or direction to reach the front wall shall not result in a hinder (and shall cause the player or team that hit the ball to lose the rally).
3) **Body Contact.** If body contact occurs which the referee believes was sufficient to stop the rally, either for the purpose of preventing injury by further contact or because the contact prevented a player from being able to make a reasonable return, the referee shall award a hinder. Body contact, particularily on the follow-through, is not necessarily a hinder.
4) **Screen Ball.** Any ball rebounding from the front wall close to the body of a player on the side which just returned the ball which interferes with or prevents the returning player or side from seeing the ball;
5) **Backswing Hinder.** Any body contact either on the backswing or en route to or just prior to returning the ball which impairs the hitter's ability to take a reasonable swing. This call may be made by the player attempting to return if it is made immediately and it is subject to acceptance and approval of the referee. Note: The interference may be construed as an avoidable hinder (See Rule 12. E.);

6) **Safety Holdup.** Any player about to execute a return who believes they are likely to strike their opponent with the ball or racquet may immediately stop play and request a dead ball hinder. This call must be made immediately and is subject to acceptance and approval of the referee. (The referee will grant a dead ball hinder if he believes the holdup was reasonable and the player would have been able to return the shot, and the referee may also determine to call an avoidable hinder if warranted.);·

7) **Other Interference.** Any other unintentional interference which prevents an opponent from having a fair chance to see or return the ball. Example: The ball obviously skids after striking a wet spot on the court floor or wall;

Rule 11. B. Effect
A call by the referee of a "hinder" stops the play and voids any situation following (such as the ball hitting the player). The only hinders a player may call are specified in Rules 11A.2), 11A.5), and 11A.6) and are subject to the acceptance of the referee. The effect of a dead ball hinder is that the player who served shall serve again, and shall be awarded two serves;

Rule 11. C. Avoidance
While making an attempt to return the ball, a player is entitled to a fair chance to see and return the ball. It is the responsibility of the side that has just served or returned the ball to move so the receiving side may go straight to the ball and have an unobstructed view of the ball after it leaves the front wall. In the judgment of the referee however, the receiver must make a reasonable effort to move towards the ball and have a reasonable chance to return the ball in order for a hinder to be called.

RULE 12. AVOIDABLE HINDERS (Point Hinder)
An avoidable hinder results in the loss of a rally. An avoidable hinder does not necessarily have to be an "intentional" act and is a result of any of the following:

Rule 12. A. Failure To Move
Does not move sufficiently to allow an opponent a shot;

Rule 12. B. Blocking
Moves into a position effecting a block on the opponent about to return the ball, or in doubles, one partner moves in front of an opponent as the partner of that opponent is returning the ball;

Rule 12. C. Moving Into The Ball
Moves in the way and is struck by the ball just played by the opponent;

Rule 12. D. Pushing
Deliberately pushes or shoves opponent during a rally;

Rule 12. E. Restricts Opponent's Swing
Moves, or fails to move, so as to restrict opponent's swing so that the player returning the ball does not have a free, unimpeded swing;

Rule 12. F. Intentional Distractions
Deliberate shouting, stamping of feet, waving of racquet, or any manner of disrupting the player who is hitting the ball;

Rule 12. G. Wetting The Ball
The players, particularily the server, have the responsibility to see that the ball is kept dry at all times. Any wetting of the ball either deliberate or by accident, that is not corrected prior to the beginning of the rally, shall result in an avoidable hinder.

RULE 13. TIMEOUTS

Rule 13. A. Rest Periods
Each player or team is entitled to three 30-second timeouts in games to 15 and two 30-second timeouts in games to 11. Timeouts may not be called by either side after service motion has begun. Calling for a timeout when none remain or after service motion has begun, or taking more than 30 seconds in a timeout, will result in the assessment of a technical for delay of game.

Rule 13. B. Injury
If a player is injured during the course of a match as a result of contact with the ball, racquet, opponent, wall, or floor, he shall be granted an injury timeout. An injured player shall not be allowed more than a total of 15 minutes of rest during the match. If the injured player is not able to resume play after total rest of 15 minutes, the match shall be awarded to the opponent(s). Muscle cramps and pulls, fatigue, and other ailments that are not caused by direct contact on the court will not be considered an injury.

Rule 13. C. Equipment Timeouts
Players are expected to keep all clothing and equipment in good, playable condition and are expected to use regular timeouts and time between games for adjustment and replacement of equipment. If a player or team is out of timeouts and the referee determines that an equipment change or adjustment is necessary for fair and safe continuation of the match, the referee may award an equipment timeout not to exceed two minutes.

Rule 13. D. Between Games
A five-minute rest period is allowed between all games of a match.

Rule 13. E. Postponed Games

Any games postponed by referees shall be resumed with the same score as when postponed.

RULE 14. TECHNICALS

Rule 14. A. Techincal Fouls

The referee is empowered to deduct one point from a player's or team's score when, in the referee's sole judgment, the player is being overtly and deliberately abusive. The actual invoking of this penalty is called a "Referee's Technical." If after the technical is called against the abusing player, and the play is not immediately continued, the referee is empowered to forfeit the match in favor of the abusing player's opponent(s). Some examples of actions which may result in technicals are:

1) Profanity. Profanity is an automatic technical and should be invoked by the referee whenever it occurs;
2) Excessive Arguing;
3) Threat of any nature to opponent(s) or referee;
4) Excessive or hard striking of the ball between rallies;
5) Slamming of the racquet against walls or floor, slamming the door, or any action which might result in injury to the court or other player(s);
6) Delay of game, either in the form of taking too much time during timeouts and between games, in drying the court, in excessive questioning of the referee on the rules, or in excessive or unnecessary appeals;
7) International front line foot faults to negate a bad lob serve;
8) Anything considered to be unsportsmanlike behavior.

Rule 14. B. Technical Warning

If a player's behavior is not so severe as to warrant a referee's technical, a technical warning may be issued without point deduction.

Rule 14. C. Effect

If a referee issues a Technical Warning, it shall not result in a loss of rally or point and shall be accompanied by a brief explanation of the reason for the warning. If a referee issues a referee's technical, one point shall be removed from the offender's score. The awarding of the technical shall have no effect on service changes or side outs. If the technical occurs either between games or when the offender has no points, the result will be that the offender's score will revert to a minus (-1).

RULE 15. PROFESSIONAL

A professional shall be defined as any player (male, female, or junior) who has accepted prize money regardless of the amount in any PRO SANCTIONED tournament (WPRA, RMA) or any other association so deemed by the AARA Board of Directors.

1) A player may **participate** in a PRO SANCTIONED tournament which awards cash prizes but will not be considered a professional if NO prize money is accepted.
2) The acceptance by a player of merchandise or travel expenses shall not be considered as prize money, and thus does not jeopardize a player's amateur status.

RULE 16. RETURN TO AMATEUR STATUS

Any player who has been classified as a professional (see Rule 15) can recover amateur status by requesting, in writing, this desire to be reclassified as an amateur. This application shall be tendered to the Executive Director of the American Amateur Racquetball Association (AARA), or his designated representative, and shall become effective immediately as long as the player making application for reinstatement of amateur status has received no money in any pro sactioned tournament, as defined in Rule 15 for the past 12 months.

RULE 17. AGE GROUP DIVISIONS

Age is determined as of the first day of the tournament:

MEN'S AGE DIVISIONS

Open — All players other than Pro
Junior Veterans Open — 19+
Junior Veterans Open — 25+
Veterans Open — 30+
Seniors — 35+
Veteran Seniors — 40+
Masters — 45+
Veteran Masters — 50+
Golden Masters — 55+
Seniors Golden Masters — 60+
Veteran Golden Masters — 65+
Advanced Golden Masters — 70+

OTHER DIVISIONS

Mixed Doubles
Disabled

WOMEN'S AGE DIVISIONS:

Open — All players other than Pro
Junior Veterans Open — 19+
Junior Veterans Open — 25+
Veterans Open — 30+
Seniors — 35+
Veteran Seniors — 40+
Masters — 45+
Veteran Masters — 50+
Golden Masters — 55+
Seniors Golden Masters — 60+
Veteran Golden Masters — 65+
Advanced Golden Masters — 70+

JUNIOR DIVISIONS

Age determined as of January 1st of each calendar year.

JUNIOR BOYS

18 & under
16 & under
14 & under
12 & under
10 & under
 8 & under (no-bounce)

Doubles Team - ages apply as above

JUNIOR GIRLS

18 & under
16 & under
14 & under
12 & under
10 & under
 8 & under (no-bounce)

SCORING — All matches in Junior divisions will be the best of two games to 15 points, win by 1 point. If a tiebreaker (third game) is necessary, the game is played to 15 points win by two points up to 21 points win by 1 point.

Junior Players should abide by all AARA rules with the following exceptions:

Rule 17. A. Eye Protection

Eye protection must be worn in all AARA junior sanctioned events.

Rule 17. B. Timeouts

Three in each game.

4 — TOURNAMENTS

RULE 18. DRAWS

a) If possible, all draws shall be made at least two days before the tournament commences. The seeding method of drawing shall be approved by the American Amateur Racquetball Association (AARA).

b) The draw and seeding committee shall be chaired by the AARA's Executive Director, National Commissioner, and the host Tournament Director. No other persons shall participate in the draw or seeding unless at the invitation of the draw and seeding committee.

c) In local, state, and regional tournaments the draw shall be the responsibility of the tournament chairperson. In regional play the tournament chairperson should work in coordination with the AARA Regional Commissioner at the tournament.

RULE 19. SCHEDULING

a) **Preliminary Matches.** If one or more contestants are entered in both singles and doubles, they may be required to play both singles and doubles on the same day or night with little rest between matches. This is a risk assumed on entering both singles and doubles events. If possible, the schedule should provide at least one hour rest period between matches.

b) **Final Matches.** Where one or more players has reached the finals in both singles and doubles, it is recommended that the doubles match be played on the day preceding the singles. This would assure more rest between the final matches. If both final matches must be played on the same day or night, the following procedure is recommended:
1) The singles match be played first.
2) A rest period of not less than one hour be allowed between the finals in singles and doubles.

RULE 20. NOTICE OF MATCHES

After the first round of matches, it is the responsibility of each player to check the posted schedules to determine the time and place of each subsequent match. If any change is made in the schedule after posting, it shall be the duty of the committee or chairperson to notify the players of the change.

RULE 21. THIRD PLACE

Players are not required to play off for 3rd place or 4th place. However, for point standings, if one semifinalist wants to play off for third and the other semifinalist does not, the one willing to play shall be awarded third place. If both semifinalists do not wish to play off for 3rd and 4th positions, then the points shall be awarded evenly.

RULE 22. AARA REGIONAL TOURNAMENTS

AARA Regional Tournaments — The United States and Europe are divided into a combined total of 16 regions.

a) A player may compete in only one regional tournament per year.

b) The defined area of eligibility for a person's region is that of their permanent residence. Players are encouraged to participate in their own region; however, for the purpose of convenience they may participate outside their region.

c) A player can participate in only two events in a regional tournament.

d) Awards and remuneration to the AARA National Championships will be posted on the entry blank.

RULE 23. TOURNAMENT MANAGEMENT

In all AARA sanctioned tournaments the tournament director and/or the National AARA official in attendance may decide on a change of court after the completion of any tournament game if such a change will accommodate better spectator conditions.

RULE 24. TOURNAMENT CONDUCT

In all AARA sanctioned tournaments, the referee is empowered to default a match if an individual player (or team) conducts him/herself (itself) to the detriment of the tournament and the game.

RULE 25. AARA ELIGIBILTY

Any paid-up AARA member in good standing, who has not been classified as a professional (see Rule 4.14) may compete in any AARA sanctioned tournament.

RULE 26. AARA NATIONAL CHAMPIONSHIP

The National Singles and National Doubles were separated and will be played on different weekends. There will be a consolation round in all divisions.

a) **Qualifying Singles.** A player may have to qualify at one of the 16 regional tournaments.

AARA REGIONS

Region 1 — Maine, New Hampshire, Vermont, Massachusetts, Rhode Island, Connecticut
Region 2 — New York, New Jersey
Region 3 — Pennsylvannia, Maryland, Virginia, Delaware, District of Columbia
Region 4 — Florida, Georgia, North Carolina, South Carolina
Region 5 — Alabama, Mississippi, Tennessee
Region 6 — Arkansas, Kansas, Missouri, Oklahoma
Region 7 — Texas, Louisiana
Region 8 — Wisconsin, Iowa, Illinois
Region 9 — West Virginia, Ohio, Michigan
Region 10 — Indiana, Kentucky
Region 11 — North Dakota, South Dakota, Minnesota, Nebraska
Region 12 — Arizona, New Mexico, Utah, Colorado
Region 13 — Wyoming, Montana
Region 14 — Nevada, California, Hawaii
Region 15 — Washington, Idaho, Oregon, Alaska
Region 16 — Americans in Europe

1) The National Ratings Committee may handle the rating of each region and determine how many players shall qualify from each regional tournament.
2) All National finalists in each division may be exempt from qualifying for the same division the following year.
3) There may be a tournament one day ahead of the National Tournament at the same site to qualify 8 players in each division who were unable to qualify or who failed to qualify in the Regionals.
4) This rule is in force only when a division is obviously over subscribed.

b) **Qualifying Doubles.** There will be no regional qualifying for doubles.

RULE 27. INTERCOLLEGIATE TOURNAMENT

It will be conducted at a separate date and location.

5 — ONE-WALL AND THREE-WALL RULES

RULE 28. ONE-WALL AND THREE-WALL RULES

Basically racquetball rules for one-wall, three-wall and four-wall are the same with the following exception:

One Wall. Court size — wall shall be 20′ in width and 16′ high, floor 20′ in width and 34′ from the wall to the back edge of the long line. There should be a minimum of three feet beyond the long line and six feet outside each side line and behind the long line to permit movement area for the players.

Short Line. Back edge 16′ from the wall.

Service Markers. Lines at least 6 inches long parallel to and midway between the long and short lines, extending in from the side lines. The imaginary extension and joining of these lines indicates the service line. Lines are 1½ inches in width.

Service Zone. Floor area inside and including the short side and service lines.

Receiving Zone. Floor area in back of short line bounded by and including the long and side lines.

Three-Wall Serve. A serve that goes beyond the sidewalls on the fly is considered "long". A serve that goes beyond the long line on a fly, but within the sidewalls is the same as "short."

Court Size, short side wall. 20′ in width and 20′ in height and 20′ in length. Side wall shall extend back on either side from the front wall parallel 20′ along the sidewall markers. Side wall may extend back 20′ at the front wall and taper down to 12′ at the end of the sidewall. All other markings are the same as the four wall.

Court Size, long side wall. 20′ in width and 20′ in height and 40′ in length. Side wall shall extend back on either side 40′. The sidewall may, but is not restricted to tapering from 20′ of height at the front wall down to 12′ at the 40′ marker. All lines are the same as in four-wall racquetball.

6 — RULES FOR 8 & UNDER NO-BOUNCE

Use AARA Racquetball rules with these modifications:

After a legal serve, the ball may bounce as many times as the receiver wants until he or she swings once to return the ball to the front wall. (In other words, the player gets one swing at the ball to get it back.)

The ball may be hit after the serve or during a rally at any time, but *must* be hit *before* it crosses the *short line* on its way *back* to the front wall.

The receiver can hit the ball before it hits the back wall or may play it off the back wall but cannot cross the short line *after* the ball contacts the back wall.

The only exception to crossing the short line is if the ball is returned to the back wall from the front wall on the fly (without touching the floor) then the receiver may cross the short line and play the ball on the first bounce.

New additions are lines on the front wall (use tape) at 3 feet and 1 foot high. If the ball is hit below the 3 foot and above the 1 foot line during a rally, it has to be returned before it bounces the third time. If the ball hits below the 1 foot line during a rally, it must be played or returned to the front wall before it bounces twice or regulation racquetball. This gives incentive to keep the ball low.

Matches are best of 2 out of 3 games to 11 points.

7 — HOW TO REF WHEN THERE IS NO REF

RULE 1 SAFETY
SAFETY IS THE PRIMARY AND OVERRIDING RESPONSIBILITY OF EVERY PLAYER WHO ENTERS THE COURT.

At *no time* should the physical safety of the participants be compromised. Players are entitled, AND EXPECTED, to hold up their swing, WITHOUT PENALTY, any time they believe there might be a risk of physical contact. Any time a player says he held up to avoid contact, even if he was over-cautious, he is entitled to a hinder (rally replayed without penalty).

RULE 2 SCORE
Since there is no ref, or scorekeeper, it is important to see that there is no misunderstanding in this area, so THE SERVER IS REQUIRED to announce both the server's and receiver's score before EVERY first serve.

RULE 3 DURING RALLIES
During rallies, it is generally the *hitter's* responsibility to make the call — if there is a possibility of a skip ball, double-bounce, or illegal hit, play should continue until the *hitter* makes the call against himself. If the hitter does not make the call against himself and goes on to win the rally, and the player thought that one of the hitter's shots was not good, he may "appeal" to the hitter by pointing out which shot he thought was bad and request the hitter to reconsider. If the hitter is sure of his call, AND the opponent is still sure the hitter is wrong, the rally is replayed. As a matter of etiquette, players are expected to make calls against themselves any time they are not sure. In other words, if a shot is very close as to whether or not it was a good kill or a skip ball, unless the hitter is sure the shot was good, he should call it a skip.

RULE 4 SERVICE
    a) **Fault Serves (Long, Short, Ceiling & Three-Wall).** The Receiver has the primary responsibility to make these calls, and again, he should give the benefit of the doubt to his opponent whenever it is close. The receiver must make his call immediately, and not wait until he hits the ball and has the benefit of seeing how good a shot he can hit. It is not an option play . . . the receiver does not have the right to play a short serve just because he thinks it's a setup.

    b) **Screen Serves.** When there is no referee, a screen serve does not become an option play. When the receiver believes his vision of the ball was sufficiently impaired as to give the server too great an advantage on the serve, the receiver may hold up his swing and call a screen serve, or, if he still feels he can make a good shot at the ball, he can say nothing and continue playing. He may not call a screen after he attempts to hit the ball. Further, the server may not call a screen under any circumstance . . . he must simply expect to have to play the rally until he hears a call from the receiver. (In doubles, unless the ball goes behind the back of the server's partner, no screens should be called.)

    c) **Others.** Foot faults, 10 second violations, receiving-line violations, service-zone infringement, and other "technical" calls really require a referee. However, if either player believes his opponent is abusing any of these rules, between rallies, he should discuss it with his opponent to be sure there is agreement on what the rule is, and to put each other on notice that the rules should be followed.

RULE 5 HINDERS
Generally, the hinder should work like the screen serve - as an option play for the hindered party. ONLY the person going for the shot can stop play by calling a hinder, and he must do so immediately - not wait until he has the benefit of seeing how good a shot he can hit. If the hindered party believes he can make an effective return in spite of some physical contact or screen that has occurred, he may continue to play. However, as safety is the overriding factor, either party may call a hinder if it is to prevent contact.

RULE 6 AVOIDABLE HINDERS
Since avoidable hinders are usually not intentional, they do occur even in the friendliest matches. When a player turns the wrong way and gets in the way of his opponent's setup, there should be a better way than saying "I'm sorry" to make up for the mistake. Instead of saying "I'm sorry", the player who realizes he made such an error should simply award the rally to his opponent. If a player feels

his opponent was guilty of an avoidable, and the player did not call it on himself, the "offended" player should appeal to his opponent by pointing out that he thought it was an avoidable. The player may then call it on himself, or disagree, but the call can only be made on yourself. Often, just pointing out what you think is an avoidable will put the player on notice for future rallies and prevent recurrence.

RULE 7 DISPUTES
If either player, for any reason desires to have a referee, it is considered common courtesy for the other player to go along with the request , and a referee suitable to both sides should be found. If there is not a referee, and a question about a rule or rule interpretation comes up, seek out the club pro or a more experienced player. Then, after the match, contact your local state racquetball association for the answer.

* Reprinted by permission of the AARA.